The Roman Stamped Tiles of Vindonissa

(1st Century A.D., Northern Switzerland)

Provenance and technology of
production – an archaeometric study

Folco Giacomini

BAR International Series 1449
2005

Published in 2016 by
BAR Publishing, Oxford

BAR International Series 1449

The Roman Stamped Tiles of Vindonissa (1st Century A.D., Northern Switzerland)

ISBN 978 1 84171 885 9

BAR Publishing is the trading name of British Archaeological Reports (Oxford) Ltd.
British Archaeological Reports was first incorporated in 1974 to publish the BAR
Series, International and British. In 1992 Hadrian Books Ltd became part of the BAR
group. This volume was originally published by Archaeopress in conjunction with
British Archaeological Reports (Oxford) Ltd / Hadrian Books Ltd, the Series principal
publisher, in 2005. This present volume is published by BAR Publishing, 2016.

Printed in England

BAR
PUBLISHING

BAR titles are available from:

BAR Publishing
122 Banbury Rd, Oxford, OX2 7BP, UK
EMAIL   info@barpublishing.com
PHONE   +44 (0)1865 310431
FAX   +44 (0)1865 316916
www.barpublishing.com

Contents

Abstract

This work presents an archaeometric study on the Vindonissa stamped tiles. Vindonissa (Canton of Aargau, Switzerland) was an important Roman camp during the 1st century AD. With Vindonissa stamped tiles, archaeologists refer to all tiles stamped with the name of the military units that were stationed at Vindonissa from 47 to 101 AD. These tiles are among the most common archaeological findings in the Vindonissa legionary camp, but commonly occur in different Roman sites of Switzerland. The first aim of this study was the petrographic and chemical characterisation of the Vindonissa tiles to determine the production site (or sites) for these ceramics and to obtain information concerning the technological aspects of the tile production and the distribution of these stamped tiles in Switzerland in Roman times.

The project was carried out in collaboration with the Archaeological service of the Canton Aargau. 217 ceramics from Northern, Central and Western Switzerland were sampled. About 20 samples from Strasbourg (France) and Rottweil (Germany) produced by the same military units of Vindonissa, as well as 15 clay samples of different provenance and data from published literature on archaeological tile productions were included in this study. The ceramic bodies and the clay samples were studied and characterised by means of petrographic, electron microprobe, X-ray fluorescence and diffraction analyses. Moreover the technical properties of the ceramics were determined by means of standard quality tests and porosimetric analyses.

To find out the production sites and the possible raw materials, the petro-chemical results were refined by a statistical data treatment including principal component and discriminant analyses. The Vindonissa tiles have heterogeneous characteristics, and can be grouped into four main groups showing good relationships to stamp types. In contrast, it is noteworthy that the groupings are not correlated with the archaeological site of provenance. This suggests that the production site (or sites) exported the tiles to different localities. Regarding the location of the production sites, there is no evidence for tile kilns at Vindonissa itself. In fact, two of the four petro-chemical groups seem to have been produced at Rupperswil and Kölliken, two Roman kiln complexes at a distance of about 20 km from the Vindonissa camp. For the other two tile groups the localisation of the production sites was uncertain.

Concerning the technological aspects of the tile production, the data suggest that the products were of mediocre quality, with weak and highly porous ceramic bodies. However, the numerous stamped tile findings at Vindonissa and in several Roman archaeological sites of Switzerland, suggest a massive tile production. This implicates a very good logistic organisation of the military workshops, if we conclude that the end-products had to be transported for dozens to hundreds kilometres to the destination localities.

Zusammenfassung

Die vorliegende Arbeit beschäftigt sich mit den gestempelten Ziegeln von Vindonissa im Kanton Aargau, Schweiz. Vindonissa war ein wichtiges römisches Legionslager im ersten Jahrhundert n. Chr. Mit dem Begriff gestempelte Ziegel von Vindonissa bezeichnen Archäologen alle Ziegel, die mit den Namen der Militäreinheiten gestempelt sind, die in Vindonissa zwischen 47 und 101 n. Chr. stationiert waren. Diese Ziegel gehören zu den häufigsten archäologischen Funden des Legionslagers. Sie werden gemeinhin aber auch in verschiedenen anderen römischen Siedlungen gefunden, die in Beziehung zum Legionslager von Vindonissa standen. Das Hauptziel dieser Studie ist die petrographische und chemische Charakterisierung der Ziegel von Vindonissa, um ihre Produktionsstätte zu bestimmen. Desweiteren soll die Untersuchung mehr Informationen über die räumliche Verbreitung der Ziegel sowie die technologischen Aspekte der Ziegelproduktion liefern.

Das Projekt wurde in Zusammenarbeit mit dem Archäologischen Dienst des Kantons Aargau durchgeführt. Insgesamt wurden 217 Keramikobjekte aus der Schweiz, sowie 20 Proben von Fundorten in Strasbourg (Frankreich) und Rottweil (Deutschland) beprobt. Die letzteren Proben wurden in die Studie einbezogen, da sie von denselben Militäreinheiten wie in Vindonissa produziert worden waren. Zudem wurden in Untersuchung weitere 15 Proben von Tonen verschiedener Herkunft sowie Literaturdaten, über römische Ziegelproduktionen berücksichtigt. Sowohl Keramikobjekte als auch Tonproben wurden petrographisch, mineralogisch und chemisch untersucht und charakterisiert. Die Untersuchungsmethoden waren Röntgenfluoreszenzanalyse und Röntgendiffraktometrie, sowie Elektronenmikrosondeanalyse. Die physikalischen Eigenschaften der Keramikobjekte wurden anhand von Standardqualitätstests und mittels Porositätbestimmung bestimmt. Um die Produktionsstätten zu lokalisieren und die möglichen Rohmaterialien zu identifizieren, wurden die petrochemischen Resultate durch statistische Datenauswertung anhand einer Hauptkomponenten- und Diskriminanzanalyse ergänzt.

Die Ziegel von Vindonissa verfügen über heterogene Eigenschaften. Sie können in vier Hauptgruppen aufgeteilt werden, welche sich mit den Stempeltypen korrelieren lassen. Die verschiedenen Gruppen können aber nicht auf die archäologischen Ursprungsorte zurückgeführt werden. Das führt zur Annahme, dass die Ziegel von einer oder mehreren Produktionstätten aus an verschiedenen Orten geliefert wurden. Die Versuche, die Produktionsstätten für diese Ziegel zu lokalisieren, erbrachte für zwei der vier petrographischen und chemischen Gruppen positive Resultate. Die Ziegel dieser zwei Hauptgruppen konnten den römischen Ziegelofenkomplexen in Rupperswil und Kölliken zugeordnet werden, welche ungefähr 20 Kilometer von Vindonissa entfernt liegen. In Vindonissa wurde kein Hinweis auf einen Ziegelofen gefunden. Die Produktionsstätte(n) der anderen zwei Ziegelgruppen konnte(n) nicht identifiziert werden.

Die Untersuchungen der physikalisch-technischen Eigenschaften ergaben, dass die Keramikprodukte aus sehr porösem Material, also von eher mittelmässiger Qualität waren. Mit Sicherheit aber weisen die zahlreichen gestempelten Ziegelfunde aus Vindonissa und anderen römischen Siedlungen der Schweiz auf eine Ziegelproduktion von riesigem Ausmass hin. Geht man von der Tatsache aus, dass die Endprodukte über mehrere Dutzende von Kilometer transportiert wurden, kann man folgern, dass die militärischen Werkstätten sehr gut organisiert gewesen sein müssen.

Resumé

Ce travail présente une étude archéométrique sur les tuiles estampillées de Vindonissa (Canton d'Argovie, Suisse). Vindonissa était un important camp militaire romain pendant le premier siècle ap. J.C. . Pour les archéologues, les tuiles estampillées de Vindonissa font référence à toutes les tuiles avec une estampille du nom des unités militaires romaines qui étaient stationnées à Vindonissa entre 47 et 101 ap. J.C.. Cestuiles sont les trouvailles plus fréquentes dans les fouilles du camp de Vindonissa, mais elles ont souvent été trouvées dans les fouilles archéologiques de divers sites suisses d'époque romaine en rapport avec Vindonissa.

Le but principal de ce travail était la caractérisation pétrographique et chimique des tuiles de Vindonissa pour pouvoir déterminer le(s) endroit(s) de production et pour obtenir des informations sur les aspects technologiques de la production tuilière et sur la distribution de ces tuiles en Suisse à l'époque romaine.

Le projet a été développé en collaboration avec le service archéologique du conton d'Argovie. 217 céramiques du Nord et de l'Ouest du la Suisse ont été échantillonnées. Cette étude inclut également 20 échantillons provenant de Strasbourg (France) et Rottweil (Allemagne) produits par les mêmes légions qu'à Vindonissa, 15 argiles de différentes provenances et des données bibliographiques sur des productions tuilières archéologiques. Les pâtes céramiques et les argiles ont été caractérisées grâce aux analyses pétrographiques, aux analyses de fluorescence et de diffraction des rayons X et aux analyses à la microsonde électronique. Les propriétés techniques des céramiques ont été déterminées avec des tests standards de qualité et avec des analyses de porosité.

Pour identifier les lieux de production et les matières premières possibles, les résultats des analyses pétrochimiques ont été traitées statistiquement par une analyse des composants principaux et une analyse discriminante.

Les tuiles de Vindonissa présentent des caractéristiques hétérogènes et elles peuvent être groupées en 4 groupes principaux qui sont liées aux types d'estampilles. Il faut remarquer que les regroupements n'ont en général pas de rapports avec le site archéologique de provenance des objets. Cette indication suggère que les tuiles aient été exportées depuis le(s) lieu(x) de production vers différents endroits. En ce qui concerne la localisation de(s) lieu(x) de production, il n'y a pas de preuve archéologique de la présence de fours tuiliers à Vindonissa. Deux des quatre groupes semblent avoir été produits à Rupperswil et Kölliken, deux complexes de fours tuiliers d'époque romaine qui se trouvent à une distance d'environ 20km de Vindonissa. Pour les deux autres groupes la localisation de(s) endroit(s) de production reste incertaine.

En ce qui concerne les aspects technologiques de la production tuilière, les données suggèrent que les produits céramiques étaient d'une qualité médiocre, avec des pâtes céramiques faibles et très poreuses. Pourtant le nombre important de tuiles éstampillées trouvées à Vindonissa et dans plusieurs sites archéologiques romains de Suisse suggère une production intensive. Ce qui implique une très bonne organisation logistique pour permettre le transport des tuiles si nous concluons qu'elles ont été exportées à des dizaines voire des centaines de kilomètres vers leur destination finale.

1. Introduction

1.1 Subject of the study

This archaeometric study deals with the military tile-production in Switzerland during the first century AD. In particular, it will focus on the tile-production related to Vindonissa, a crucial military outpost at the border of the Roman Empire in the first century AD (Fig. 1.1). A large number of tiles, stamped on the upper surface with the name of the producing military unit, were found during archaeological excavations of the military camp as well as in a number of other archaeological sites in Switzerland.

The majority of the tiles studied are *tegulae*. They are the only tiles with stamps and therefore can be attributed to a legionary production. Tegulae are large, flat tiles with raised lateral margins. As depicted in Fig. 1.2, they were put close together and composed the main cover of a

Roman roof (Jahn, 1909). A few frontal tiles or *antefixa* have also been examined (fig. 1.3b/c), because these decorated tiles are typical for "official" or public buildings and are likely related to military productions. The half-rounded pantiles or *imbrices* have not been analysed, since they are not stamped and their attribution to a military production is impossible.

1.2 History of the Vindonissa military camp

This section gives a brief introduction of the history of the legionary camp at Vindonissa (and its strategic importance) during the first century AD. For a complete review on the history of Vindonissa, refer to Hartmann (1986) and Fellman (1988).

Founded under Tiberius by the 13th legion *gemina* in the second decade AD, Vindonissa had at the beginning of the century a merely defensive character. The camp occupied a strategic position at the confluence of three

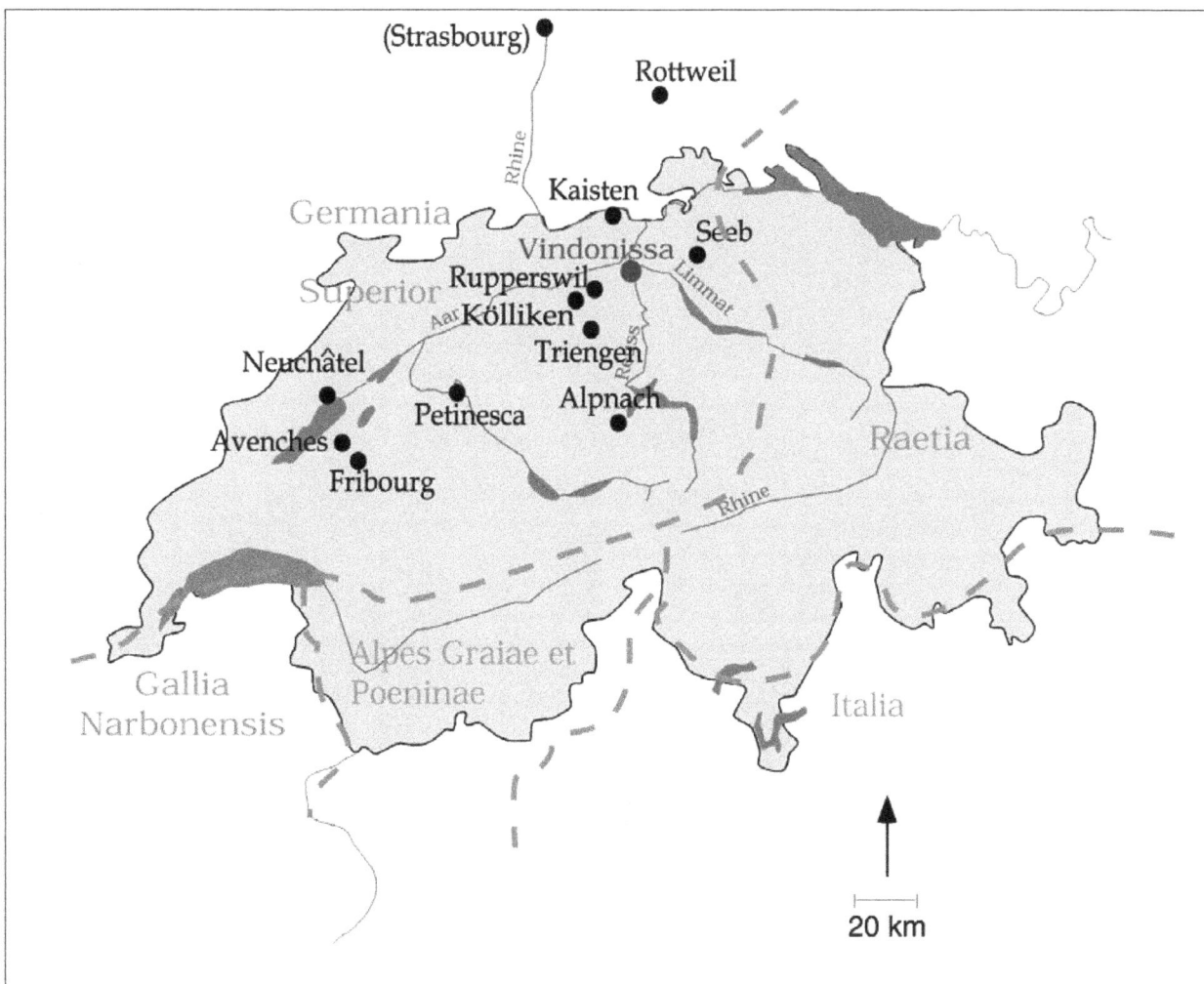

Fig. 1.1: The location of the Vindonissa legionary camp and the province subdivision between the 1st and 3rd Century AD. Modified from Drack (1975). The main archaeological sites cited in the work are also reported.

3

important rivers, the Aar, the Limmat and the Reuss (fig. 1.1). This consented to control the main access to the Swiss plateau and, in later times, to the Alpine passes in the South. During this first phase, the camp was probably constructed in wood and there is no evidence of extensive tile production at the site.

The change of the imperial foreign policy from the year 45 AD, during the reign of the emperor Claudius, led to a series of changes at Vindonissa. The 13th legion had moved to Poetovio (Yugoslavia) and the 21st legion *rapax* arrived at Vindonissa probably in the year 47 AD (Hartmann, 1986). The old camp was enlarged and the buildings renewed in stone and brick. During this period, a huge tile-production is attested. Through the presence of stamped tiles we know that some auxiliary cohorts were stationed at Vindonissa in support of the 21st legion (Hartmann and Speidel, 1991). Following the archaeological interpretations the 7th cohort *Raetorum* and the 26th cohort *voluntariorum civium Romanorum* were the first present at Vindonissa. They were later replaced by the 3rd cohort *Hispanorum* and by the 6th cohort *Raetorum*. Both cohorts stayed at Vindonissa together with the 21st legion until the year 69 AD. The importance of Vindonissa was growing and the camp changed its role from a defensive outpost to a starting point for the beginning expansion of the Roman Empire towards southern-western Germany. Stamped tiles on findspots along the Upper Rhine Valley, including Strasbourg, prove for the presence of detachments of the 21st legion. During this phase, the camp could have accommodated about 6000 soldiers, but the troops never were in full strength in Vindonissa.

In the year 70 AD, after defeating the adherents of Vitellius, the 21st legion left Vindonissa and was sent by Vespasianus to southern Germany to stop the revolt of the Bataves (Tacitus, Historiae 1,67-69). At the beginning of the year 71 AD the 11th legion *claudia pia fidelis* was moved from Burnum (Dalmatia) to Vindonissa. This legion most likely occupied the camp until the year 101 AD, when Traianus moved it to the region of the lower Danube. During the occupation by the 11th legion *claudia pia fidelis*, the legionary camp was partially rebuilt. A huge quantity of stamped-tiles and other ceramic products attests this reconstruction phase. At that time Vindonissa was still an important military base, which was also involved in the expansion to southern-western Germany. The importance of Vindonissa declined only when the 11th legion moved on to a troop camp near Rottweil. This camp seemed to have become the new starting point for further campaigns towards the Neckar Valley (Franke, 1998).

1.3 Stamps classification

All the analysed tiles except two samples from Vindonissa and the *antefixa* are stamped on their upper surface (fig. 1.3a) with the name of the producing military unit (legion or cohort).

A number of different stamps have been reported for the tiles produced by the legions based at Vindonissa. Victor Jahn's study (1909), up to the present day, is the most complete work on these stamps. It includes a large number of hand-drawn tables reporting the characteristics of each stamp: its shape, the type of inscription, the shape of the letters etc.

This author was able to identify at least 77 different stamp shapes for the Vindonissa military units, which he grouped into 16 main types (Jahn, 1909). Eight of these types could be attributed to the 21st legion, three were produced by the 11th legion and 5 types are products of the cohorts. Annexe A provides all the Jahn's tables with the stamp classification, which have until now never been entirely published. The original tables were kindly provided by the Vindonissa Römer Museum in Brugg.

Unless otherwise stated, I will always refer to Jahn's classification to identify the analysed stamped tiles.

1.3.1 Stamp shape and inscriptions

All stamps of the two legions, except three types (Jahn 12,13 and 14) have the common shape of the *tabula ansata* and all report the shortened name of the producing military unit (see fig.1.3a and annexe A).

Tiles of the Cohorts and of the 11th legion display commonly one type of inscription (LEG·XIC·PF = 11th *legio claudia pia fidelis* or C·VII·R = 7th *cohors Raetorum*). In contrast, the stamps of the 21st legion are more complex. The most common stamps have abbreviated inscriptions such as L·XXI (Jahn 1,2,11,13) or LEG·XXI (Jahn 9). Anyway, different inscriptions, such as L·XXI·L (Jahn 12), L·XXIC· (Jahn 4) and L·XXI·S·C·VI (Jahn 3) are also present. With respect to some archaeological interpretations there is no agreement on the meaning of the different suffixes "L", "C" and "S·C·VI".

A short summary of the main archaeological interpretations for the suffixes is here reported:

- Stamp type 4 - L·XXIC·:

1) Fuchs and Margueron (1998) suggest that the suffix C, followed by a little dot, could represent an ancient name of the legion, like in the stamps of the 11th legion (LEG·XIC·PF)

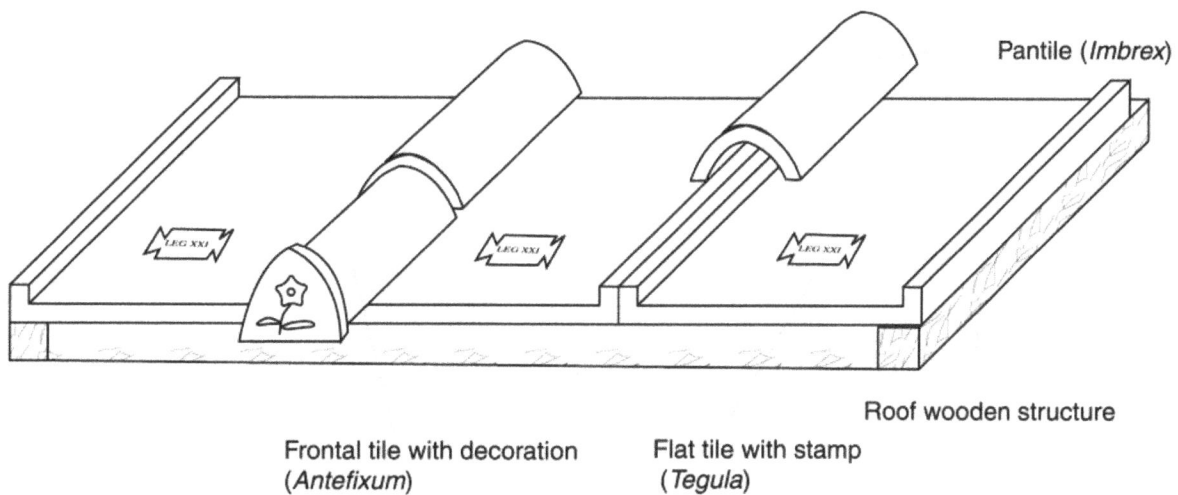

Fig. 1.2: Simplified schema of a Roman roof. A timber structure props up ceramic flat tiles (*tegulae*), which are joined together by pantiles (*imbrices* and *antefixa*). One tegula is about 50-55 cm long, 38-42 cm wide and 3-4 cm thick. Its weight is on average 11 kg (data from Jahn, 1909).

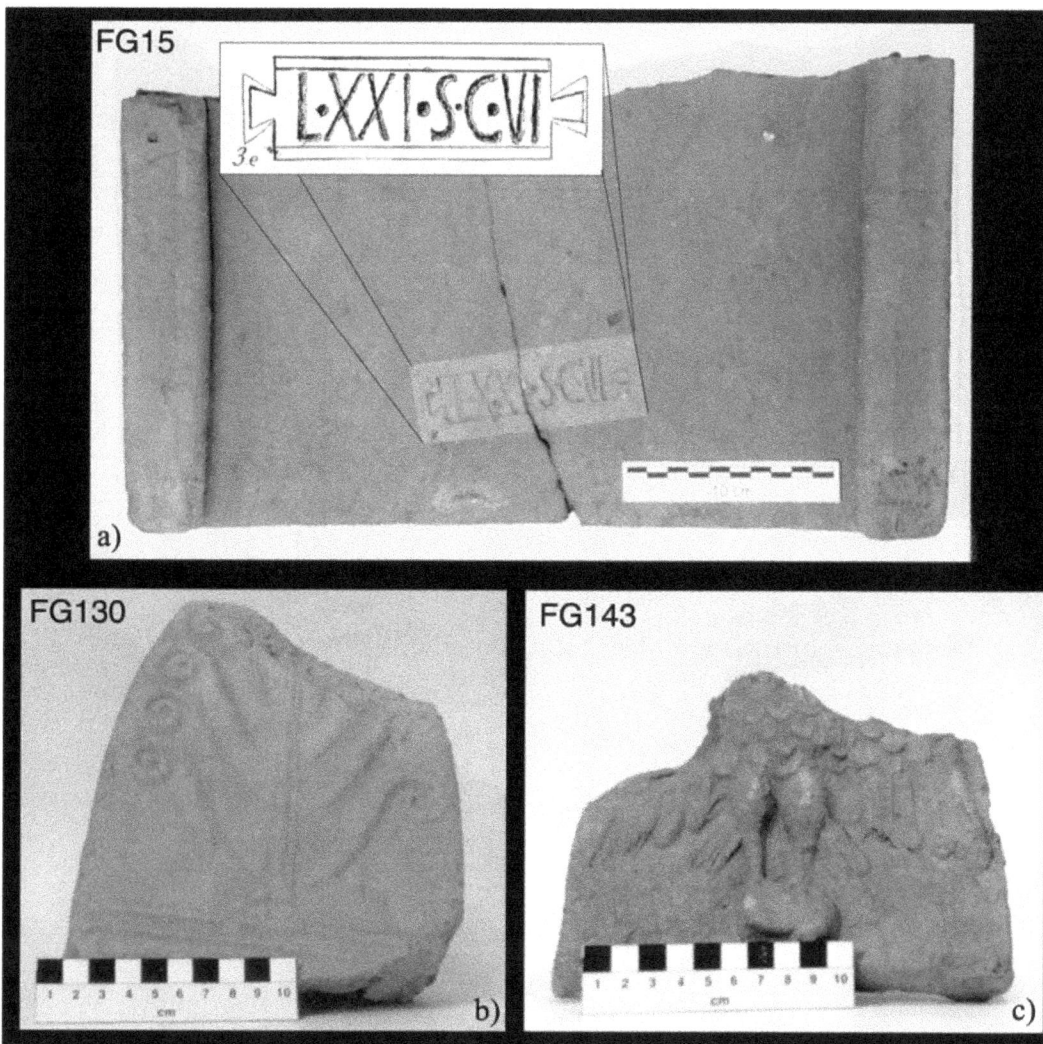

Fig. 1.3:a) Sample FG15, *tegula* from Vindonissa legionary camp. Following Jahn's classification (1909), the tile reports a stamp of type 3e (highlighted). One of the original Jahn's drawings is also reported in the figure. b), c) *Antefixa* from Vindonissa, with ornamental bas-reliefs of a plant (FG130) and of an imperial eagle (FG143).

5

fabricae as proposed by Le Bohec (1989) or of the *centurio Fabrum* (Jahn, 1909), i.e. the person responsible for the production. In this case "C" would probably indicate a name (Caius?).

3) According to Steinby (1978) "L·XXIC·" could mean *l(egione) XXI c(urante)* .

- Stamp type 12 - L·XXI·L : As for the previously discussed suffix Le Bohec (1989) and Jahn (1909) interprete the suffix "L" as the abbreviated name of either the *magister fabricae*, or a *centurio fabrum* : "L" would then indicate a name (Lucius?).

- Stamp type 3 - L·XXI·S·C·VI : the suffix "S·C·VI" has three different interpretations.

1) According to Jahn (1909) S·C·VI stands for *sub cura Victoris*. His interpretation states for the presence of a person, which was directly responsible for the production.

2) Bohn (1925) suggests *sub castris Vindonissensibus.* He argues that this could indicate the presence of (private?) workshops, which worked under the control of the legionary camp.

3) The third interpretation by Howald and Meier (1940) is *sagittarum cohortis VI.*

Finally, stamps LXXIR, with the R probably meaning *rapax* do not appear in the classification of Jahn: this stamp is found on one sample only, found in Strasbourg (FG228).

In the next sections different terms are used to identify groups of stamp types and groups of samples. These simplified terms are reported below to avoid confusion:

-The first group is referred to as *Vindonissa stamps*: this designation applies for all the 16 stamp-types identified by Jahn (1909) for the tiles of the two legions and auxiliary cohorts, which were found at Vindonissa and in the other Swiss archaeological sites.

-The term *Vindonissa tiles* indicates all the tiles reporting

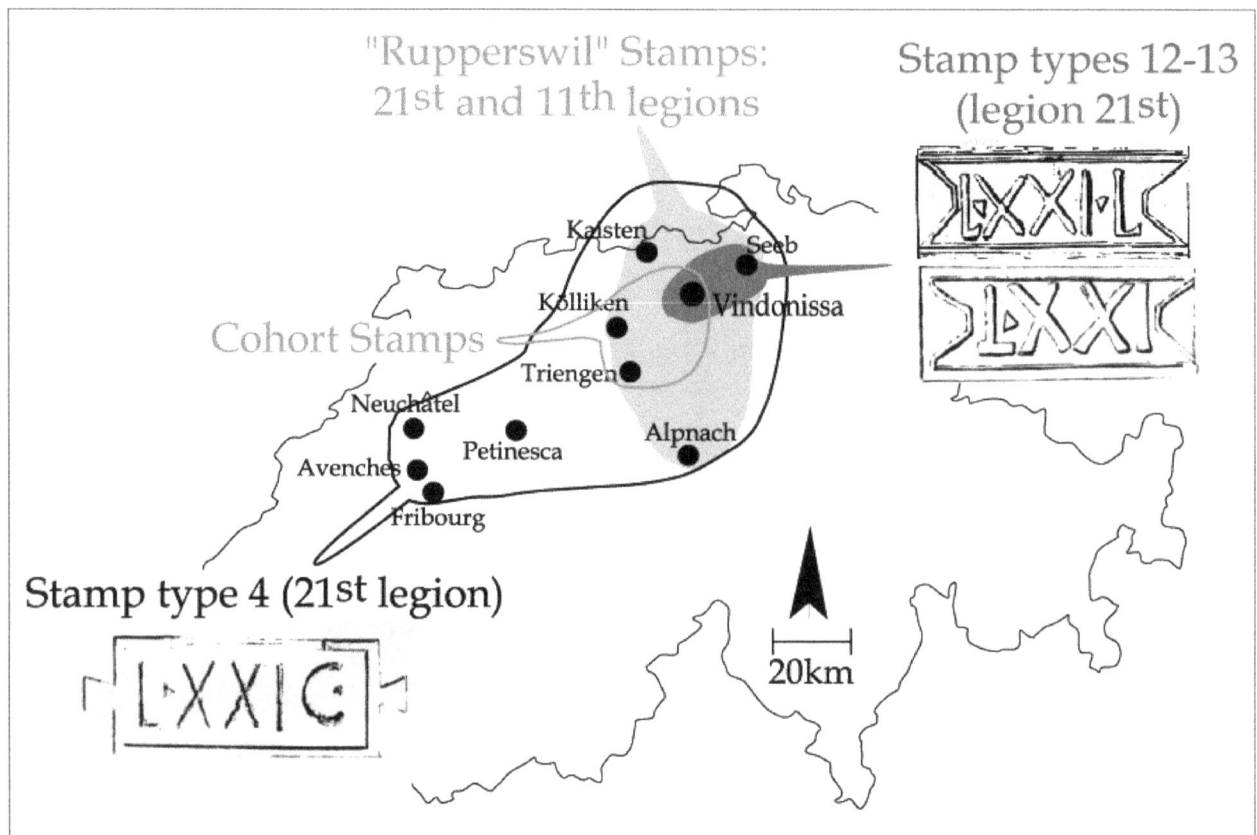

Fig. 1.4: Schematic map of the stamp-type distribution in Northern and Western Switzerland. Stamp types, or groups of stamp types, have different geographic distributions. The stamp reproductions are from Jahn (1909), see Annexe A.

one of the Vindonissa stamps.

-The *Rupperswil stamps* represent a subgroup of *Vindonissa stamps*. This subgroup is formed by stamps occurring in the Rupperswil tile kiln (Arnold, 1965). As explained in the next paragraph, only stamp-types 1,2,3,9,11 for the 21st legion and 14,15,16 for the 11th legion were found during the archaeological excavation of the Rupperswil kiln.

-The *Rupperswil tiles* are those tiles having one of the Rupperswil stamps.

1.3.2 Distribution of the stamp-types

Several authors provided distribution maps and concepts, which demonstrate that the Vindonissa tiles are widespread in Switzerland.

Von Gonzenbach (1963) has drawn a detailed schema of the distribution of tiles of the 21st and 11th legions: she underlines that all the findings concentrate along the main Roman military road. She further states that all the findings are linked up to military outposts or military-related buildings. Conversely, on the basis of the new findings and of an accurate study of their distribution, Fuchs and Margueron (1998) hypothesise that the findings of stamped tiles are not only confined to military buildings, but are often found in religious as well as civilian buildings. Moreover Fuchs and Margueron (1998) observed that in the westernmost Roman sites of Switzerland (Avenches, Neuchâtel, Fribourg, Petinesca) stamp type 4 (L·XXIC·) is virtually the only stamp type present. Just one tile with stamp type 3 (L·XXI·S·C·VI) has been found in the sanctuary "Grange des Dîmes" at Avenches. On the contrary, up to the present day, no stamps of the 11th legion were found in any of the western Swiss sites.

Concerning Central and Eastern Switzerland, all published data agree in that there is a certain correspondence among stamp-type frequencies and archaeological sites. Within the military camp of Vindonissa only all tile types are present.

Cohorts stamps were found in few sites in Central Switzerland: Vindonissa, Kölliken and Triengen (Arnold, 1965; Hartmann and Speidel, 1991; Fetz and Meyer-Freuler, 1997). Some tiles of the 21st legion have also a limited distribution, concentrating between Vindonissa and sites in East Switzerland. Stamp-types 12 (L·XXI·L) and 13 (L·XXI) were found, until now, only in Vindonissa and Seeb, close to a Roman *villa rustica* (Drack, 1987).

Finally, the tiles of the 11th legion *claudia pia fidelis* are generally present only in Central and Eastern Switzerland. Following the interpretation of Von Gonzenbach (1963), the lack of tiles of the legion *claudia* in the West is due to the weakening strategic importance of the West at the end of the 1st century AD and due to the abandoning of its military settlements. Figure 1.4 is a simplified map of the distribution of the stamp-type in Switzerland. The distribution map is based on data from the literature and from information collected during the sampling.

1.4 The tile kilns

The problem of the location of the production site (or sites) for the Vindonissa tiles, is still a matter of debate. Archaeological excavations have revealed the presence in Central Switzerland of at least 18 tile kilns (Le Ny, 1998), which were active between the 1st and the end of the 3rd century AD. No kilns were found at Vindonissa itself or in the proximity of the military camp. This is somewhat astonishing since the region around the site provides the raw materials (clay), water and also wood fuel for an intensive ceramic production. Yet in the 19th century there were some tile factories active in the region around Brugg (Letsch, 1907), about 3-4 km away from the ancient camp. Only four of the 18 excavated kilns seem to be related to the Vindonissa legions (fig. 1.5). These are the kilns at Rupperswil, Kaisten, Kölliken and Triengen.

In Roman times, the nearest kiln that might have been used by the two legions for their brick production is that of Rupperswil (AG), which was found in 1963/64 during the construction of the highway A1 Bern-Zürich (Arnold, 1966). Archaeologists agree on the importance of this production centre, with several kilns concentrated in an area of about 20000 m² and is located at a distance of approximately 20 km from Vindonissa. About 120 stamped fragments of both legions and a large number of unstamped fragments were found during the excavation. A considerable number of the tiles are overfired, often deformed and commonly interpreted as wasters (Arnold, 1966). During the first century AD at least, the site was the main production centre for Vindonissa tiles, but possibly not the only one (Fellmann, 1988). In fact, as noticed by Arnold (1966), not all stamp types reported by V. Jahn (1909) for Vindonissa tiles are found at Rupperswil. The lacking stamps belong all to the production of the 21st legion *rapax* (Jahn 4, 12 and 13) and of its auxiliary cohorts (Jahn 6, 7, 8, 10). In contrast, the types of the 11th legion *claudia pia fidelis* are all represented in Rupperswil. It is therefore likely that all the bricks and tiles of the 11th legion were produced in the Rupperswil workshop (Arnold, 1966).

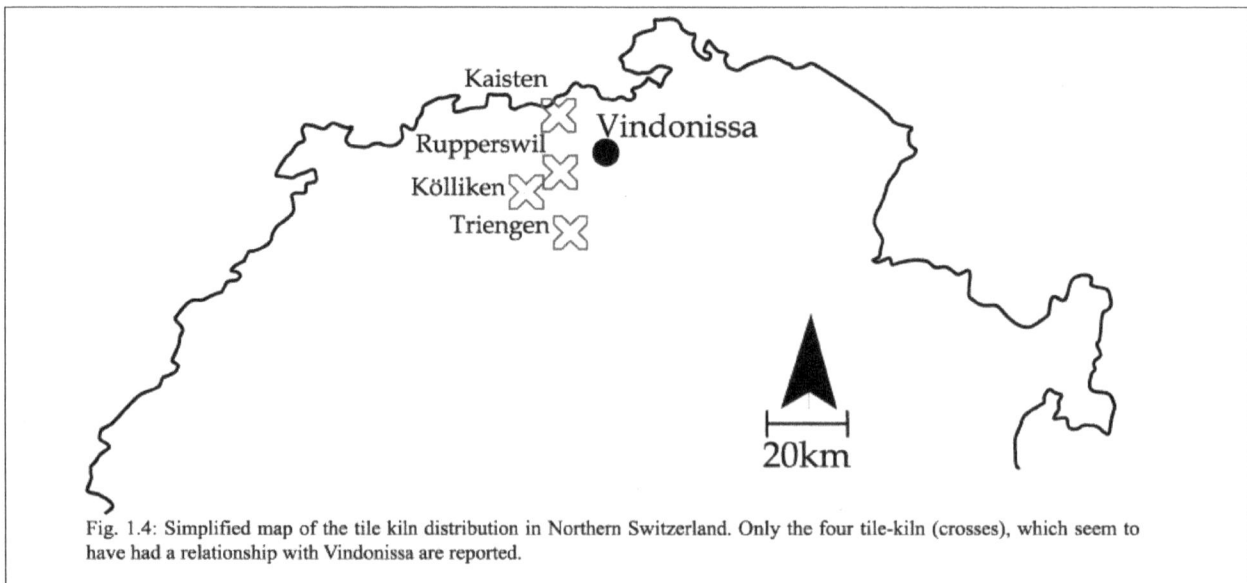

Fig. 1.4: Simplified map of the tile kiln distribution in Northern Switzerland. Only the four tile-kiln (crosses), which seem to have had a relationship with Vindonissa are reported.

Three other kilns, Kölliken (AG), Kaisten (AG) and Triengen (LU), were recently excavated (Le Ny, 1998). Some stamped tiles were found in the kiln walls of the complexes of Kölliken and Kaisten, but this might not indicate that stamped tiles were really produced here. The presence of stamped tiles in the kiln walls could also be a sign of recycling of older products. There is no agreement about the function of the kiln at Kölliken. According to Hartmann and Speidel (1991), it represents a production site of the 21st legion and of some cohorts, whereas Hardmeyer et al. (1993) assume that the kiln was used during the 2nd and 3rd century AD, after the departure of the Roman legions.

Archaeological data suggest that the kiln of Triengen was used by neither of the two legions. A large number of stamped tiles were found in the archaeological complex of Triengen, but all finds are related to a *villa rustica*. No stamped tiles were found near the tile kiln. Moreover, the unstamped tiles found near the kiln have remarkable differences in the dimensions, when compared to the stamped ones (Fetz and Meyer-Freuler 1997).

1.5 Archaeometric studies on military tiles

Although military stamped tiles commonly occur frequently in Roman archaeological sites, only few contributions deal with the military productions in the Germania superior province (see fig.1.1). The works, which to my knowledge, deal with this argument are reported below:

-        Maggetti and Galetti (1994): analyses on the stamped tiles of the 1st legion *Martiorum*, stationed in Augusta Raurica in later Roman times. The authors pointed out that the production of the 1st legion *Martiorum*

is rather homogeneous, and that it is most likely of local origin, although there is no certainty about the raw material used.

-        Dolata (2000): analyses on stamped tiles from Mainz (Germany), production of the 21st legion *rapax* ; this work has an archaeological approach, principally and it is implemented with a series of chemical analyses on archaeological samples, but no hypotheses are proposed for the provenance and the raw materials of these ceramics.

-        Schneider (personal communication, work in progress, 2001): analyses on the stamped tiles from Rottweil (Germany), production of the 11th legion *claudia pia fidelis*;

-        the British archaeometric school, proposes a number of works on the brick and tile production of the Roman military units in Great Britain. Most of them deal with the technological aspects of the tile production as well as with the quantification of the production and will be considered in chapter 7 of this work.

1.6 Aims of the work

The Vindonissa stamped tiles have been subject of archaeological studies for nearly a century (Jahn, 1909; Von Gonzenbach, 1963; Arnold 1966). They are often cited in new archaeological publications on Roman settlings of Switzerland.

The "Vindonissa tiles" are one of the most common finds not only in Vindonissa, but also in a number of other Swiss archaeological sites. It is noteworthy that the Vindonissa stamped tiles have been found at sites, which

8

are dozens to hundred kilometres away from Vindonissa (fig. 1.4).

Goal of this work was to answer some questions regarding the tile production related to Vindonissa legionary camp and to produce new data useful for the archaeological interpretations. The main questions arising from the "Vindonissa tiles" problem, are shortly reported here.

a) Is the whole Swiss production homogenous? Is it possible to distinguish among the productions of the different military units (21st and 11th legions, cohorts)? If the productions are heterogeneous, could the differences in stamp types indicate for the presence of different workshops or different artisans responsible for the production?

To answer these questions, a large number of tiles of all the military units found at Vindonissa was first analysed. For comparison, analyses were carried out on ceramics of the same military units, which were found in other archaeological sites in Switzerland. The ceramic bodies were studied and characterised by means of modal petrographic analyses, X-ray fluorescence and diffraction analyses as well as electron microprobe analyses (see annexe B for details).

b) Where are the production sites located?

Although Vindonissa appears to be the centre from which the tile production started (Jahn, 1909), at present the archaeological excavations did not bring to light any evidence of workshops or tile kilns in the legionary camp. One of the aim of this study was to locate the production site (or sites) for the tiles found at Vindonissa by comparing the chemo-petrographic characteristics of the tiles with those of the local clays. The chemo-petrographic characterisation of the ceramics and clays was perfectioned by statistical data treatment (principal component and discriminant analysis)

c) Can the "Vindonissa tiles" be distinguished from other similar productions in the Germania Superior province?

To further improve the comparison of the results of Vindonissa tiles, I analysed few samples of the 21st legion from Strasbourg (France) and some tiles and pots of the 11th legions from Rottweil (Germany). Moreover, other data and publications on stamped tiles were included in the study. In particular the data of Maggetti and Galetti (1994), Dolata (2000) and Schneider (personal communication) were taken as comparison.

d) What was the level of technological skill of the Roman craftsmen? Did they use particular techniques in the tile

fabrication? Is the quality of their ceramics comparable to that of modern products?

With respect to the technological aspects of the tile fabrication I focused attention on questions regarding the clay processing and the firing conditions as well as the quantification of the tile production for the Vindonissa camp. Finally I compared the quality of Roman tiles to that of modern tile products by performing standard quality tests on the archaeological samples.

With this work, I attempt to provide new data for the interpretation of the distribution of the tiles in Switzerland during the Roman imperial age. The results of my investigations should contribute to a better understanding of the role the Roman military units played in Switzerland.

2. Sampling strategy

The sampling strategies are briefly reported in this paragraph. For the analytical strategies and procedures, see the Annexe B.

217 ceramics coming from different archaeological sites have been sampled. 203 of these were studied from a chemical and a petrographical point of view. The larger part of the objects is represented by stamped tiles (*tegulae*) of the production of the 21st and 11th legions and of the auxiliary cohorts. Annexe C reports the complete list of samples, with their provenance and principal characteristics.

The tiles come both from Vindonissa (103 samples) and other archaeological sites. The goal was to collect a representative number of samples for each stamp type from all the sampling sites. The sampling sites were chosen as a function of their geographical position: Fribourg, Neuchâtel, Alpnach, Petinesca, Seeb, Strasbourg and Rottweil (see also fig. 1.1) represent the locations furthest away from the camp of Vindonissa, in which several finds of stamped tiles are attested. One stamped tile from Rupperswil, considered a waster because of its strong deformation and the presence of vitrified parts was also sampled and analysed.

Table 2.1 reports the number of tiles sampled from each archaeological site and the relative number for each stamp types. It is possible to notice that the number of samples changes from site to site. This depends just on the sample availability: the goal was to collect the largest number of samples from each locality, in order to have a statistically significant sampling. Unfortunately, the number of stamped tiles in several archaeological sites is very esiguous. From Vindonissa, 17 frontal tiles (*antefixa*) and two tiles without stamp were also collected. The latter are two isolated finds coming from an archaeological layer of Augustean age, i.e. they are older than the legionary camp. For this period, no buildings with a tile-roof are attested in Vindonissa and archaeologists are interested to know whether it is possible to attribute the two unstamped tiles to a local production.

Moreover, 18 "legionary pots" of the 11th legion's production were collected: these pots are typical of the Vindonissa area (Ettlinger, 1998; Ettlinger and Simonnet, 1952). Following archaeological interpretations, they were produced in place, although no kiln was found in the camp. 13 of these pots come from Vindonissa, and five from Rottweil (Germany), where a similar production is attested. From Rottweil, it was possible to sample three tiles of the 11th legion, which display stamp types similar to those attested in Vindonissa.

For the comparison between final products and possible raw materials, I collected 15 clay samples from different localities, which were considered possible production sites, based on the archaeological data. The clays were sampled at a depth of 1-2 meters, which corresponds to the average depth of the Roman archaeological finds in the region. To have a wider spectrum of clays, 18 analyses of clay samples of already published works were considered. Complete information relative to the clay samples (name, sampling locality, geological formation) is reported in chapter 6.

Archaeological site of provenance	Stamped tiles Stamp Types (Jahn, 1909)																Tiles with not classified stamps	Unstamped tiles	Total n° of samples
	1	2	3	4	5	6	7	8	9	10	11	12	13	14	15	16			
Alpnach	1	3	2	1	-	-	-	-	1	-	-	-	-	2	2	1	-	-	13
Avenches	-	-	1	9	-	-	-	-	-	-	-	-	-	-	-	-	-	-	10
Fribourg	-	-	-	2	-	-	-	-	-	-	-	-	-	-	-	-	-	-	2
Kaisten	-	1	2	1	-	-	-	-	-	-	-	-	-	2	2	-	-	-	8
Neuchâtel	-	-	-	1	-	-	-	-	-	-	-	-	-	-	-	-	-	-	1
Petinesca	-	-	-	3	-	-	-	-	-	-	-	-	-	-	-	-	-	-	3
Rottweil	-	-	-	-	-	-	-	-	-	-	-	-	-	-	-	-	3	-	3
Rufenach	1	-	-	-	-	-	-	-	-	-	-	-	-	-	-	-	-	-	1
Rupperswil	-	-	-	-	-	-	-	-	-	-	-	-	-	-	-	1	-	-	1
Seeb	-	4	7	2	-	-	-	-	-	-	-	15	3	-	1	2	-	-	34
Strasbourg	-	-	-	-	-	-	-	-	-	-	-	-	-	-	-	-	3	-	3
Vindonissa	9	9	7	13	4	2	2	2	7	4	1	6	5	10	10	7	3	2	103
Total	11	17	19	32	4	2	2	2	8	4	1	21	8	14	15	11	9	2	182

Table 2.1: list of the analysed tiles grouped following their stamp type and their archaeological site of provenance.

3. Petrography

3.1 The tiles

The observation of thin sections allowed the distinction of five main petrographic fabrics among the tiles of the two legions and of the auxiliary cohorts. This grouping relates commonly to stamp types. Petrographic distinction criteria were mainly the texture and the composition of the clay matrix, the modal percentage and the shape of non-plastic inclusions, argillaceous rock-fragments (ARFs) and pores (as explained in annexe B.2).

As concerns Vindonissa tiles, the mixtures are generally coarse-grained, often with a high percentage of a silt-component in the matrix. They display a rather heterogeneous distribution of the non-plastic inclusions, which are commonly subangular. The observed fabrics

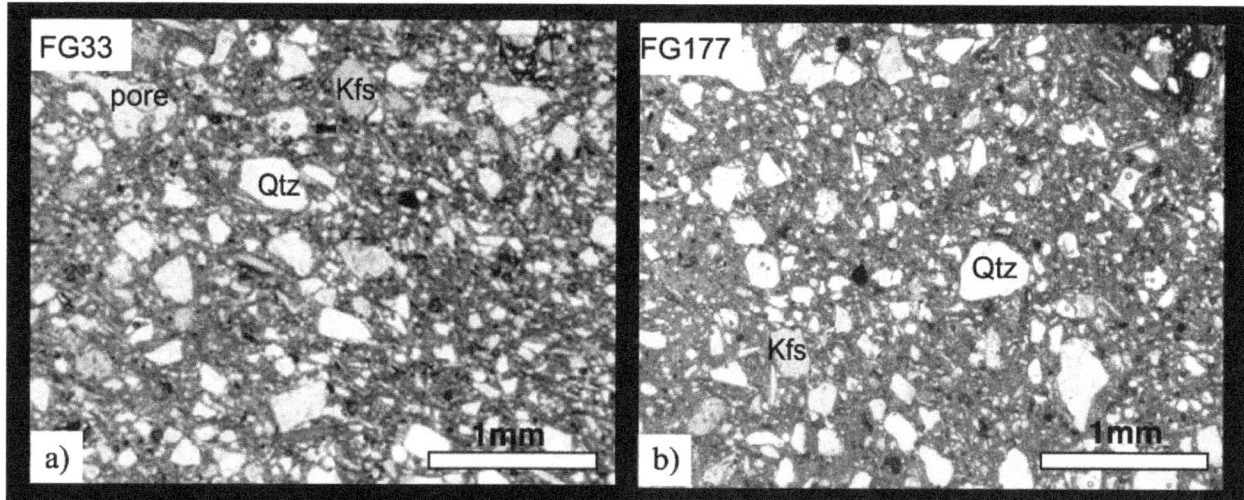

Fig. 3.1: a), b) Photomicrographs of representative samples belonging to the petrographic fabric "a". Both samples report a stamp of type 12 (L·XXI·L);c)High-magnification photomicrographs of sample FG33 (stamp type 12): it is still possible to recognise the sheet structure of the original clay minerals in the matrix.

Fig. 3.2: Photomicrographs at different scales of sample FG203, fabric "b" (stamp type 13). The clay source is not homogeneous and it is composed by a calcareous and a silt-rich clay. The square in a) represents the zoomed area in photo b).

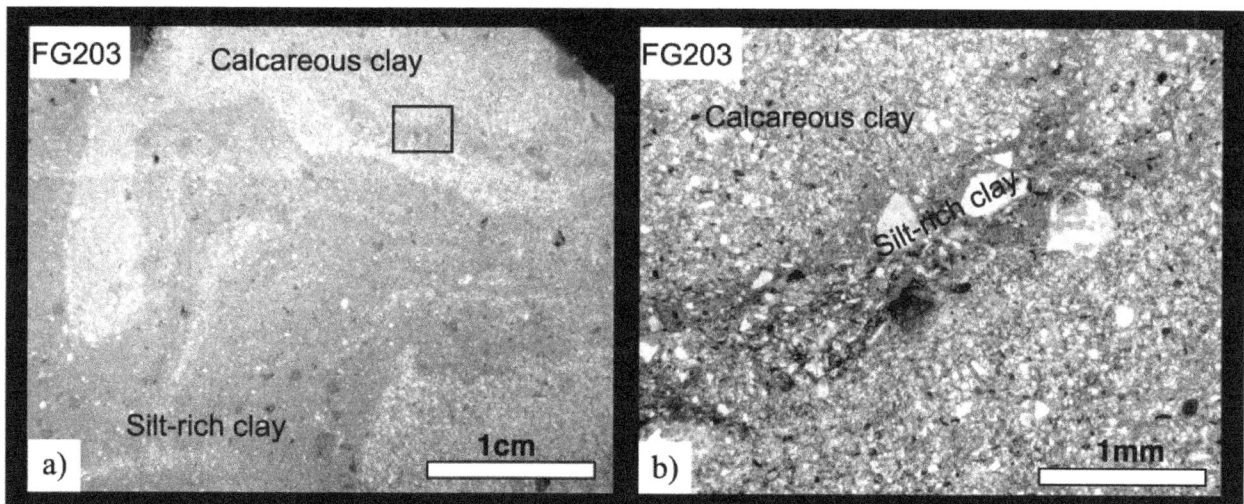

suggest that for the majority of the tiles, young sediments were used.

Sub-rounded pebbles (up to 1.5-2 cm in diameter) and large argillaceous rocks fragments scattered throughout the ceramic bodies were often observed.

Photomicrographs of the five main petrographic fabrics are shown in figures 3.1 to 3.5. Table 3.1 reports the classification of the samples into different fabric types. In Annexe D the results of petrographic point-counting analyses made on 35 tile samples are reported. The petrographic analyses suggest that the samples are not strongly contaminated. The internal surface of the pores commonly does not have concretions of secondary minerals, with the exception of very rare discontinuous rims of secondary calcite. Their estimated volume percentages were always below any petrographic significance.

3.1.1 Petrographic fabric "a"

This first petrographic fabric, regroups the majority of tiles with stamp-type 12. Three tiles, whose stamps could not be attributed because of bad preservation (FG25, -33 and -115) also fall into this first fabric group. For these three samples, archaeological observations suggest two possible stamp types: 12 or 13. Macroscopically, the tiles with this fabric type are commonly light-red to orange coloured, the ceramic paste is soft and it can be pulverised easily. The ceramic body has a sand-silty texture (fig. 3.1a/b) and is rich in white-mica flakes. The non-plastic inclusions are angular to sub-angular and range between 15 and 18 vol%. The dimensions of the non-plastic inclusions range from 0.05 to 0.4 mm in diameter. Quartz is largely the major component, followed by K-feldspar, with percentages varying from 1 to 2 vol%. ARFs are commonly absent, or only present as minor constituents. Microscopic porosity is in the range 1.4-3 vol%. Clay minerals in the matrix and white mica preserve their interference colours and do not display

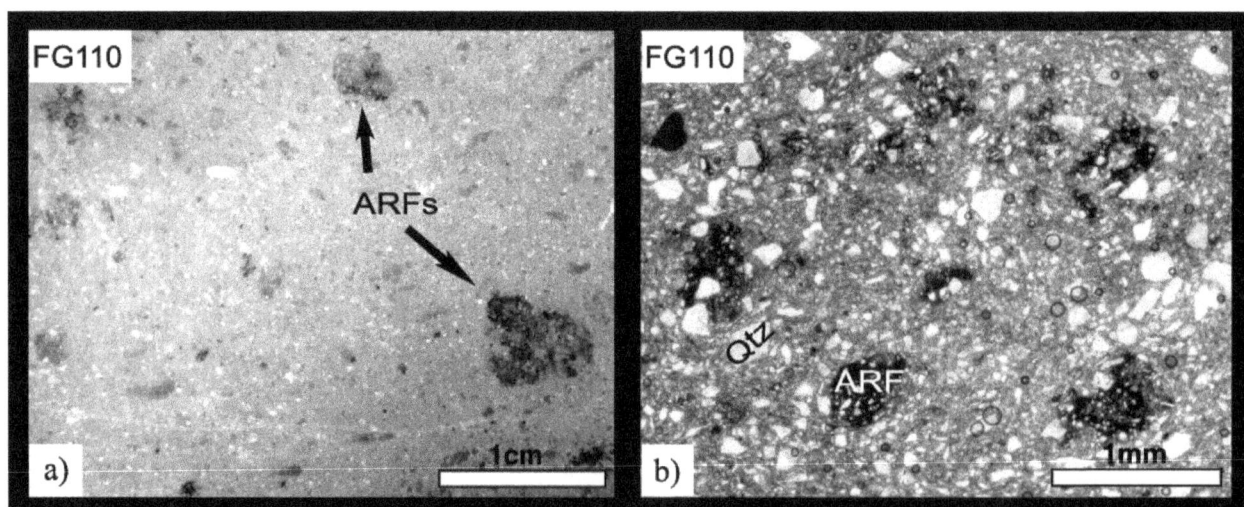

Fig. 3.3: Photomicrographs at different scales of sample FG110, fabric "c" (stamp type 6). Large amounts of dark-brown ARFs with a greywacke texture, are present: a) Photo at the mesoscale; b) Photo at the microscale.

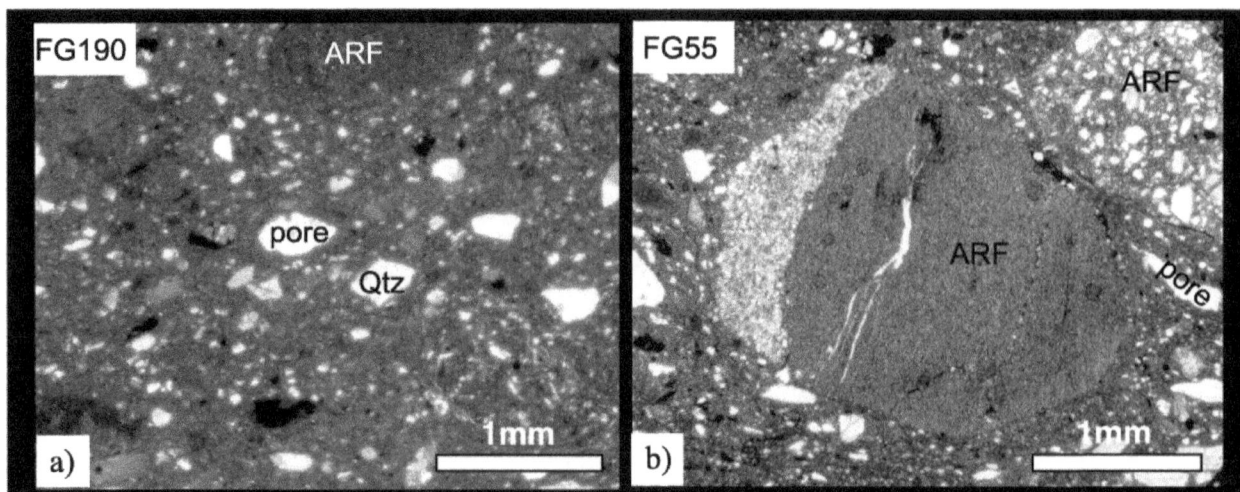

Fig 4: Photomicrographs of fabric "d" tiles. a) Sample FG190 stamp type 4; b) Sample FG55, stamp type 9. The ceramic body are relatively clay-rich and large argillaceous rock fragments (ARFs) are widespread.

strong evidence of firing-induced oxidation or sintering (fig. 3.1c).

3.1.2 Petrographic fabric "b"

The second family is formed by the very rare tiles with stamp type 13. Macroscopically, these tiles are orange to beige coloured and display a complex "cloudy" fabric, made up of thin layers of two different clays that are chaotically mixed (fig 3.2a). The ceramic body is relatively soft and the surface is of the tiles is often strongly altered. Under the microscope, the ceramic body is commonly fine-grained and the matrix is composed of a mixture of a calcareous and a non-calcareous silt, the latter being very similar to the matrix of fabric "a" (fig. 3.2b). The percentage of the two different matrices is strongly variable from sample to sample. However, the tiles are commonly easy to distinguish, because of their complex cloudy texture. White-mica flakes are frequent accessories. The non-plastic inclusions constitute about 5 vol% and their dimensions follow a hiatal distribution: small, rounded grains (0.02-0.1 mm) clearly predominate on larger, sub-angular ones (0.4-0.5 mm). Quartz grains and calcite fragments or limestone fragments predominate over the other non-plastic inclusions, which are present only as accessory phases. ARFs are absent. Microscopic porosity ranges between 2 and 3.2vol% As well as in the previous family, these tiles show low sintered ceramic bodies. Clay minerals as well as the calcite fragments always preserve their optical properties, demonstrating that their crystalline structure is still present after firing.

3.1.3 Petrographic fabric "c"

This fabric is frequent in the tiles of the Cohorts production and in the frontal tiles (*antefixa*). In contrast, it is very rare among tiles of legion 21st (only three samples from Vindonissa: FG11, FG22 and FG99) and completely absent in 11th legion's tiles. The ceramic body is orange to reddish, it appears well sintered and has a good hardness. The main feature of this fabric is the presence of large, dark-brown inclusions easily recognisable on the macroscopic sample and giving it a heterogeneous, spotted look (fig.3.3a). Under the

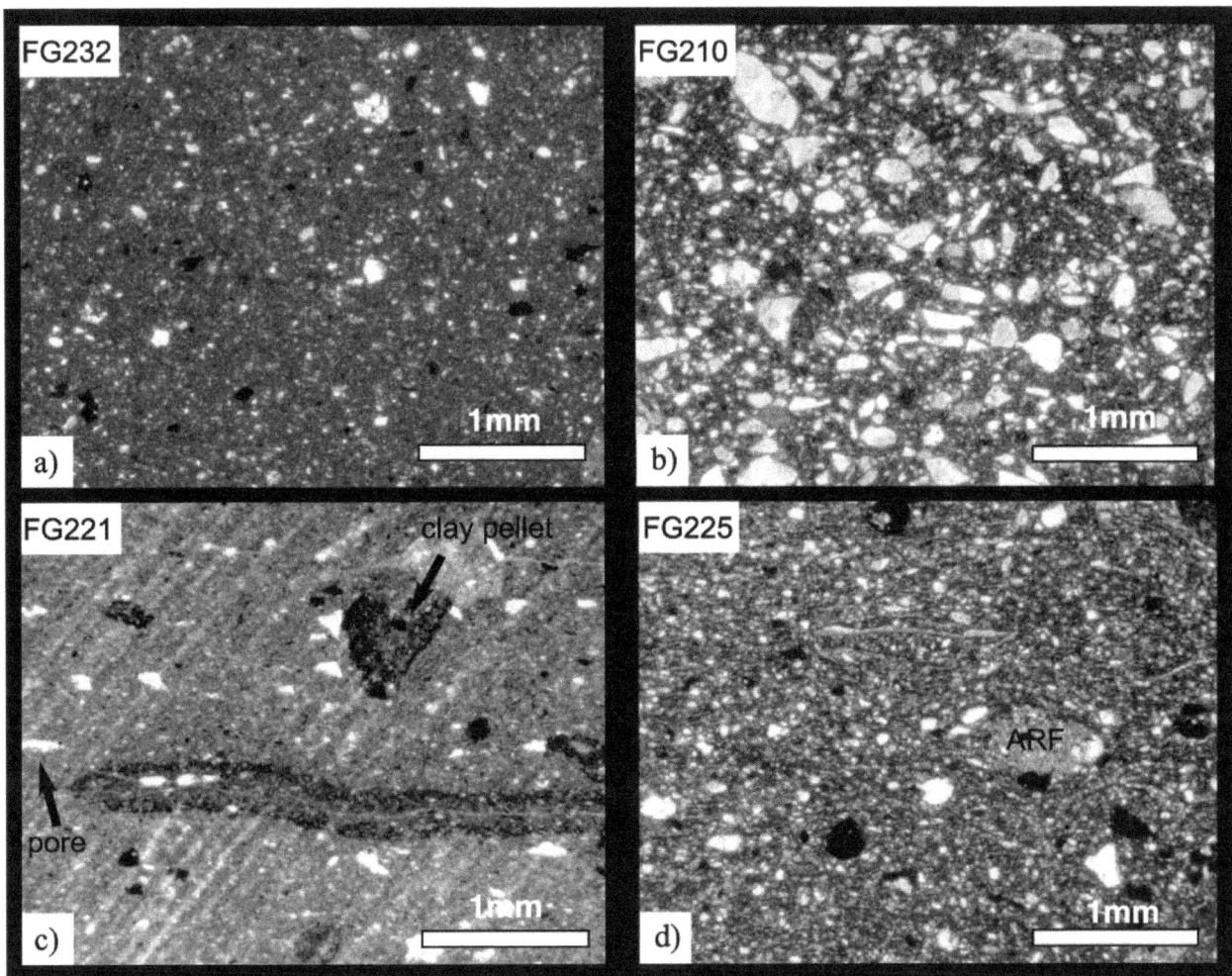

Fig. 3.5: Photomicrographs of tile and pottery samples. a) Sample FG232, stamped tile from Rottweil (11th legion). b) Sample FG210, legionary pot from Vindonissa (11th legion) displaying a sandy texture. c), d) samples FG221 and FG225 respectively, legionary pots from Rottweil, attributed to the 11th legion. This last shows a good resemblance with the tile from Rottweil (photo a) and a clear textural difference with the pots from Vindonissa (photo b).

microscope, the inclusions (up to 20vol%) appear as argillaceous fragments (ARFs) with a greywacke texture (fig.3.3b). The ceramic body is coarse grained and composed by a silt-rich mixture. The non-plastic inclusions (0.3-0.5mm) reach up to15 vol% and are quartz-dominated. White mica flakes are small and dispersed as accessory in the matrix. The ARFs are typically richer in the clay component than the surrounding matrix and they do not display any internal structure. This suggests that they are not grog fragments (Whitbread, 1986; Cuomo di Caprio and Vaughan, 1993).

3.1.4 Petrographic fabric "d"

The fourth petrographic family represents the majority of the "Vindonissa tiles". These samples are generally red to wine-red coloured. Their ceramic body is usually hard and resistant to scratching. Under the microscope, the textures display wide modal variations. The non-plastic inclusions range between 5 and 15 vol% and ARFs between 1.5 and 7vol%. Among the non-plastic inclusions, quartz is the most common phase (up to 13vol%), followed by K-feldspar and Na-rich plagioclase (the latter never over 1vol%). Biotite flakes, epidote grains and well-rounded limestone grains are common accessory phases, whereas white-mica flakes are rarely present.

The ARFs distribution shows the prevalence of large (up to 3mm), brown clay pellets and rounded greywacke fragments (fig. 3.4a). Rounded silt fragments are only sometimes present. In rare cases, ARFs are composite: clay may grade towards silt and silts towards greywacke (fig. 3.4b). The microscopic porosity is in average slightly higher than that observed in the previous families (3-8%). This feature can be attributed to the higher modal amounts of ARFs, which during firing behave as plastic inclusion and thus undergo an intense shrinking.

Clay minerals and micas in the matrix show a wide range of textures. In some specimens, it is not possible to recognise them any more, since the ceramic body is very well sintered. This feature is rather common in tiles with stamp type 4 (L·XXIC·), as shown in figure 3.4c/d.

3.1.5 Petrographic fabric "e"

The three tiles from Rottweil (samples FG232, FG237, FG238) are rather different from the Vindonissa tiles. The ceramic body is composed by a fine-grained silty matrix, with accessory clay pellets and rare (< 1 vol%) non plastic inclusions of size 0.2-0.4 mm (fig. 3.5a, next page). The non-plastic grains are generally sub-rounded. Compared to the tiles from Vindonissa, those of Rottweil seem to be made with a much more evolved natural sediment, with high percentage of fine grained clay minerals and low percentage of well-rounded non plastic inclusions.

3.2 Petrography of the pottery

The legionary pots from Vindonissa (samples FG208 to FG220) are coarse ceramics, displaying a texture very similar to that of petrographic fabric "a". The ceramic bodies are sand-rich with angular non-plastic inclusions up to 0.4 mm (fig. 3.5/b).

The legionary pots from Rottweil (three thin sections analysed: FG221, FG222, FG225) have different textures, which are easily comparable to the textures of the tiles from Rottweil. FG221 and FG222 are very fine-grained ceramics with few non-plastic inclusions (< 1 vol%) of 0.2-0.4mm in diameter. Clay pellets (0.1-0.5mm) are common accessory constituents. The samples show a high microscopic porosity characterised by thin, sub-parallel pores (fig. 3.5c).

Sample FG225 is coarser than the other pots from Rottweil, but if compared to the coarse ceramics of Vindonisssa, the non-plastic inclusions of sample FG225 are smaller in size and more rounded (fig. 3.5d).

Table 3.1: Sample classification after petrographic analysis. Five main petrographic fabrics have been identified.

Fabric	Sample ID	Stamp-type	Military Unit	Fabric	Sample ID	Stamp-type	Military Unit	Fabric	Sample ID	Stamp-type	Military Unit
a	FG23	12	21st legion	c	FG35	6	7th cohort	d	FG34	5	6th cohort
a	FG24	12	21st legion	c	FG37	10	3rd cohort	d	FG38	5	6th cohort
a	FG25	12-13?	21st legion	c	FG39	8	26th cohort	d	FG41	Rupp. Stamps	21st legion
a	FG33	12-13?	21st legion	c	FG40	7	7th cohort	d	FG47	4	21st legion
a	FG36	12	21st legion	c	FG57	10	3rd cohort	d	FG48	4	21st legion
a	FG74	12	21st legion	c	FG59	10	3rd cohort	d	FG49	4	21st legion
a	FG96	12	21st legion	c	FG61	10	3rd cohort	d	FG50	5	6th cohort
a	FG174	12	21st legion	c	FG77	8	26th cohort	d	FG51	Rupp. Stamps	21st legion
a	FG176	12	21st legion	c	FG98	6	7th cohort	d	FG52	Rupp. Stamps	21st legion
a	FG177	12	21st legion	c	FG110	7	7th cohort	d	FG53	Rupp. Stamps	11th legion
a	FG178	12	21st legion	c	FG130	-	-	d	FG54	Rupp. Stamps	11th legion
a	FG179	12	21st legion	c	FG131	-	-	d	FG55	Rupp. Stamps	21st legion
a	FG180	12	21st legion	c	FG132	-	-	d	FG62	Rupp. Stamps	21st legion
a	FG181	12	21st legion	c	FG134	-	-	d	FG63	Rupp. Stamps	21st legion
a	FG182	12	21st legion	c	FG99	Rupp. Stamps	21st legion	d	FG64	Rupp. Stamps	21st legion
a	FG196	12	21st legion	d	FG12	Rupp. Stamps	21st legion	d	FG65	Rupp. Stamps	21st legion
a	FG201	12	21st legion	d	FG13	Rupp. Stamps	21st legion	d	FG66	Rupp. Stamps	21st legion
a	FG202	12	21st legion	d	FG14	Rupp. Stamps	21st legion	d	FG67	Rupp. Stamps	11th legion
a	FG204	12	21st legion	d	FG15	Rupp. Stamps	21st legion	d	FG68	Rupp. Stamps	11th legion
a	FG205	12	21st legion	d	FG16	4	21st legion	d	FG69	Rupp. Stamps	11th legion
a	FG206	12	21st legion	d	FG17	4	21st legion	d	FG70	Rupp. Stamps	21st legion
a	FG207	12	21st legion	d	FG18	4	21st legion	d	FG72	5	tile coh
b	FG71	13	21st legion	d	FG19	4	21st legion	d	FG73	Rupp. Stamps	21st legion
b	FG75	13	21st legion	d	FG20	Rupp. Stamps	21st legion	d	FG76	Rupp. Stamps	21st legion
b	FG90	13	21st legion	d	FG21	Rupp. Stamps	21st legion	d	FG78	Rupp. Stamps	11th legion
b	FG91	13	21st legion	d	FG26	Rupp. Stamps	11th legion	d	FG79	Rupp. Stamps	11th legion
b	FG95	13	21st legion	d	FG27	Rupp. Stamps	11th legion	d	FG80	Rupp. Stamps	11th legion
b	FG175	13	21st legion	d	FG28	Rupp. Stamps	11th legion	d	FG81	Rupp. Stamps	11th legion
b	FG200	13	21st legion	d	FG29	Rupp. Stamps	11th legion	d	FG82	4	21st legion
b	FG203	13	21st legion	d	FG30	Rupp. Stamps	11th legion	d	FG83	4	21st legion
c	FG11	Rupp. Stamps	21st legion	d	FG31	Rupp. Stamps	11th legion	d	FG84	Rupp. Stamps	21st legion
c	FG22	Rupp. Stamps	21st legion	d	FG32	Rupp. Stamps	11th legion	d	FG85	4	21st legion

Rupp. Stamps, Rupperswil Stamps

Table 3.1 - continued : Sample classification after petrographic analysis. Five main petrographic fabrics have been identified.

Fabric	Sample ID	Stamp-type	Military Unit
d	FG86	4	21st legion
d	FG87	Rupp. Stamps	21st legion
d	FG88	Rupp. Stamps	11th legion
d	FG89	Rupp. Stamps	21st legion
d	FG92	Rupp. Stamps	11th legion
d	FG93	Rupp. Stamps	11th legion
d	FG94	Rupp. Stamps	11th legion
d	FG100	Rupp. Stamps	21st legion
d	FG101	Rupp. Stamps	21st legion
d	FG102	Rupp. Stamps	11th legion
d	FG103	Rupp. Stamps	21st legion
d	FG104	Rupp. Stamps	11th legion
d	FG105	4	21st legion
d	FG106	4	21st legion
d	FG107	Rupp. Stamps	21st legion
d	FG108	Rupp. Stamps	21st legion
d	FG109	Rupp. Stamps	21st legion
d	FG111	Rupp. Stamps	11th legion
d	FG112	Rupp. Stamps	11th legion
d	FG113	Rupp. Stamps	11th legion
d	FG114	Rupp. Stamps	11th legion
d	FG116	Rupp. Stamps	21st legion
d	FG118	Rupp. Stamps	11th legion
d	FG119	Rupp. Stamps	21st legion
d	FG120	Rupp. Stamps	21st legion
d	FG121	Rupp. Stamps	11th legion
d	FG122	Rupp. Stamps	11th legion
d	FG123	Rupp. Stamps	11th legion
d	FG126	-	-
d	FG133	-	-
d	FG135	-	-
d	FG140	Rupp. Stamps	11th legion

Fabric	Sample ID	Stamp-type	Military Unit
d	FG144	4	21st legion
d	FG145	4	21st legion
d	FG146	4	21st legion
d	FG147	4	21st legion
d	FG148	4	21st legion
d	FG149	4	21st legion
d	FG151	4	21st legion
d	FG152	4	21st legion
d	FG153	4	21st legion
d	FG154	4	21st legion
d	FG155	4	21st legion
d	FG156	4	21st legion
d	FG157	4	21st legion
d	FG158	4	21st legion
d	FG159	4	21st legion
d	FG160	4	21st legion
d	FG161	Rupp. Stamps	21st legion
d	FG162	4	21st legion
d	FG163	Rupp. Stamps	11th legion
d	FG164	Rupp. Stamps	11th legion
d	FG165	Rupp. Stamps	21st legion
d	FG166	Rupp. Stamps	21st legion
d	FG167	Rupp. Stamps	21st legion
d	FG168	Rupp. Stamps	21st legion
d	FG169	Rupp. Stamps	11th legion
d	FG170	Rupp. Stamps	11th legion
d	FG171	Rupp. Stamps	11th legion
d	FG172	Rupp. Stamps	21st legion
d	FG173	Rupp. Stamps	21st legion
d	FG183	Rupp. Stamps	11th legion
d	FG184	Rupp. Stamps	21st legion
d	FG185	Rupp. Stamps	21st legion

Fabric	Sample ID	Stamp-type	Military Unit
d	FG186	Rupp. Stamps	21st legion
d	FG187	Rupp. Stamps	21st legion
d	FG188	Rupp. Stamps	21st legion
d	FG189	Rupp. Stamps	21st legion
d	FG190	4	21st legion
d	FG191	Rupp. Stamps	21st legion
d	FG193	Rupp. Stamps	21st legion
d	FG194	Rupp. Stamps	11th legion
d	FG195	Rupp. Stamps	11th legion
d	FG197	4	21st legion
d	FG199	Rupp. Stamps	21st legion
e	FG232	?	11th legion
e	FG237	?	11th legion
e	FG238	?	11th legion

Rupp. Stamps, Rupperswil Stamps

Table 3.2: The uncertain or unclassified samples after petrographic analyses

Sample n°	Stamp Type	Military Unit	Fabric
FG10	Stamps Rupp.	21st legion	d?
FG56	Stamps Rupp.	21st legion	a?
FG58	Stamps Rupp.	21st legion	?
FG60	12	21st legion	a-b?
FG97	Stamps Rupp.	21st legion	?
FG115	12-13?	21st legion	a-b?
FG117	Stamps Rupp.	21st legion	d?
FG141*	-	-	?
FG142*	-	-	?
FG143**	-	-	d?
FG150	Stamps Rupp.	21st legion	a?
FG198	Stamps Rupp.	21st legion	a?
FG226	Stamp Strasbourg	21st legion	not analysed
FG227	Stamp Strasbourg	21st legion	not analysed
FG228	Stamp Strasbourg	21st legion	not analysed

Rupp. Stamps, Rupperswil Stamps

4. Chemistry

In this section, the results of the chemical analyses of all the studied ceramic samples are presented. The section starts from a comparison of the chemical composition of stamped tiles belonging to different fabrics to test the hypothesis that the petrographic classification is also reproduced in the chemical composition of the tiles. Finally, a comparison among the chemical compositions of the production of the different military units and of the other ceramic samples (unstamped tiles and legionary pots) will be undertaken. In the Annexe E the chemical compositions of the analysed samples are reported.

Before interpreting the chemical analyses, it was necessary to evaluate the amount of contamination of the archaeological samples and the sample reproducibility. As explained in Annexe B3, archaeological objects may undergo contamination processes during the long burial in the soil. For this reason the behaviour of chemical elements which may be affected by the contamination processes (leaching and precipitation by percolating fluids), were carefully controlled (see Annexe B3). The chemical data suggest that contamination is commonly low for the analysed ceramics. P_2O_5 is commonly in the range 0.07-0.49 wt%, except in the case of nine samples, which have P_2O_5 concentration higher than 0.5 wt%. To discard the contamination effect, these nine analyses were recalculated with the average phosphorous content of the other samples, as explained in the Annexe B3. Commonly it was possible to observe that the sample reproducibility was rather good. In addition, the differences among two specimens of the same samples were not significant if compared to the differences observed between different groups of samples.

4.1 The "Vindonissa tiles"

The majority of "Vindonissa tiles" are Ca-poor ceramics. Their chemical compositions are not homogeneous in both major and trace elements. The concentrations of SiO_2 and Al_2O_3, vary through the dataset approximately of 20 and 12 wt%, respectively. Some trace elements have relative variations higher than 100%. By looking at the binary diagrams in figure 4.1, the whole set has an internal structure and the elemental distribution of the samples shows good correlation with the petrographic fabric. In figure 4.1 the samples with uncertain petrographic fabric are labelled . Only samples FG58 and FG150 have strongly peculiar characteristics and are easily distinguishable from the other samples, as shown in fig. 4.1b and f.

Tiles classified into petrographic fabric "a" form a quite homogeneous group, which lies always marginally with respect to the large scatter formed by the majority of the samples (fig. 4.1a,b, e, f). These ceramics have high SiO_2/Al_2O_3 ratios and relatively low alkali and MgO

contents. The high SiO_2 concentration relates to the quartz-rich ceramic bodies of this group of tiles. The tiles of fabric "b" (stamp-type 13 s.s.) are the most different from the average composition of the Vindonissa tiles. However, the small sample number (n=8) reduces the possibility of clear interpretation. Nevertheless it is possible to observe that these eight samples have rather heterogeneous compositions, and commonly display high CaO and low Al_2O_3, Fe_2O_3, K_2O and Na_2O contents. The positive correlation between Al_2O_3 and SiO_2, contrasting with the general trend of the other samples, is probably due to the mixing of two clays in different proportions. The chemical data suggest that one of the mixed clays is similar to that of the tiles of fabric "a". Actually, all the samples plot along a mixing line connecting the field of tiles with fabric "a" with a hypothetical Ca-rich end-member (fig 4.1a, b, c, d). The tiles of the fabric "c", which are characterised by the presence of dark-brown clay pellets, are homogeneous and differ from the other tiles, mainly due to the lower MgO and CaO contents and higher Na_2O/K_2O ratios. Finally, the tiles classified into fabric "d" form a large, heterogeneous group (not outlined with a coloured field). It is interesting to observe that the three frontal tiles classified into this fabric (FG126, FG133, FG135), plot near the field of tiles with fabric "c". Fig 4.2 is a scatter plot from tiles classified into fabric "d" only, in which the objects are labelled according to their stamp types. In particular, the Rupperswil stamps (types 1,2,3,9,14,15 and 16) were distinguished from the stamp type 4 (L·XXIC·). The entire group forms a large, heterogeneous cloud of points. Figure 4.2 shows that about half of the tiles with a stamp L·XXIC· are chemically comparable with those forming the Rupperswil group, although they often occupy a marginal position with respect to the remaining samples. The other half (13 samples) differs both in their major and trace element contents. These 13 tiles stamped L·XXIC· (FG16, FG17, FG18, FG19, FG48, FG146, FG149, FG152, FG153, FG154, FG158, FG159, FG190) have particularly high MgO, Ni and Cr concentrations.These concentraqtions of Ni and Cr are nearly twice as high as those of the remaining tiles of petrographic fabric "d" (fig. 4.1 and 4.2). There is no petrographic evidence for the high contents of these three elements, whose concentrations are therefore most likely related to the clay matrix and not to a-plastic inclusions of mafic mineral or rock fragments. Moreover, it is noteworthy that there is no correlation between this chemical composition and the provenance of these objects: actually, tiles with high Cr and Ni contents are found in Vindonissa as well as in Seeb and at the Western Swiss sites.

For a wider spectrum of compositions that can be compared with this group, a number of published data on archaeological ceramics from Switzerland were studied. As shown in Duruz and Maggetti (1997), Hertli et al.

(1999) and Maggetti and Galetti (2001) high contents in Ni and Cr are only found in Switzerland in ceramics coming from Reinach (BS) and from the Rhône valley between Martigny and Genève. In the latter cases, the

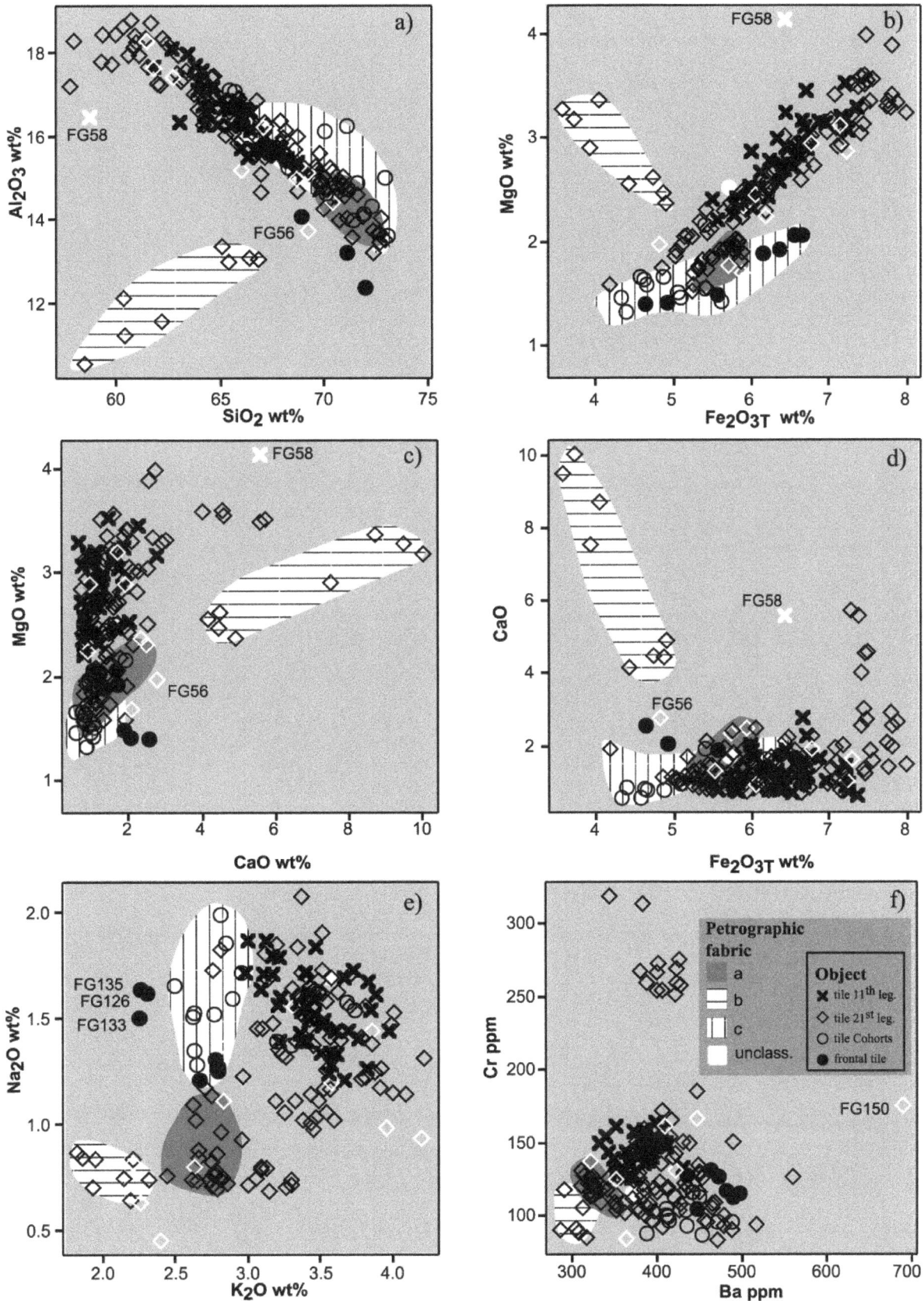

Fig. 4.1: Bivariate chemical diagrams for the ensemble of "Vindonissa tiles". The data set shows an internal structure with a rather good correspondence with the petrographic fabrics. tiles with petrographic fabric "d" represent the main point scatter, not labelled for simplicity,

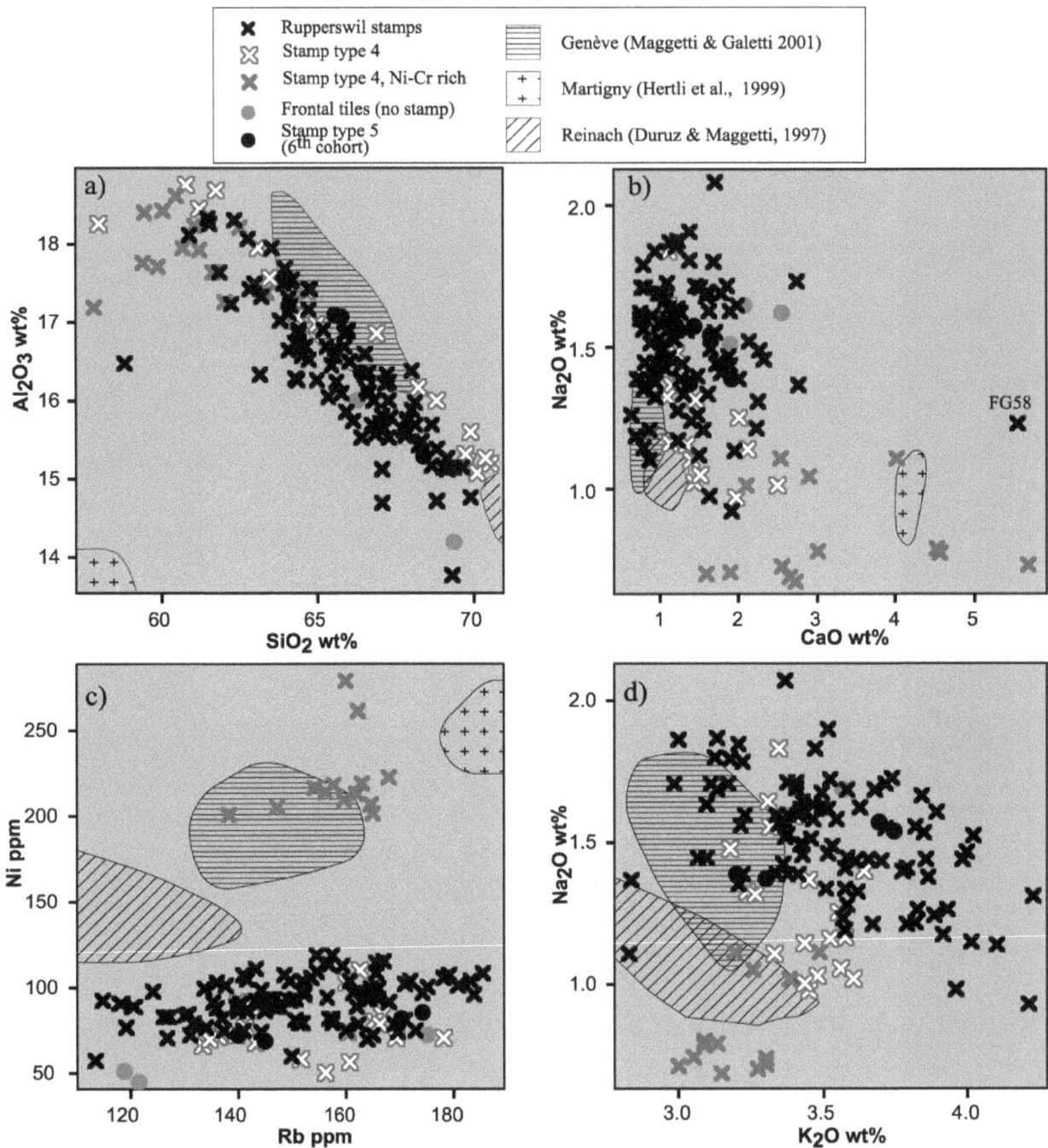

Fig.4.2: Bivariate chemical diagrams showing only the tiles of petrographic fabric "d". The samples are labelled following their stamp types. The tiles with stamp type 4 (L.XXIC.) lie often in a marginal position with respect to the other tiles with fabric "d" and 13 samples display very different Ni (and Cr, fig. 4.1f) contents. Fields for three published Swiss reference groups characterised by high Ni and Cr contents are also reported for comparison. None of the three reference groups rich in Ni and Cr is comparable with the 13 tiles of stamp type 4.

influence of the ophiolitic Alpine nappes is most likely at the basis of such high Ni and Cr values in the clays. In fig. 4.2 the compositional fields of ceramics from Martigny, Genève and Reinach are reported for comparison.

Finally, Figures 4.3 and 4.4 show the chemical composition of Cohort- and frontal-tiles, respectively. Both productions split into two distinct chemical groups, with a good correspondence with the petrographic classification.

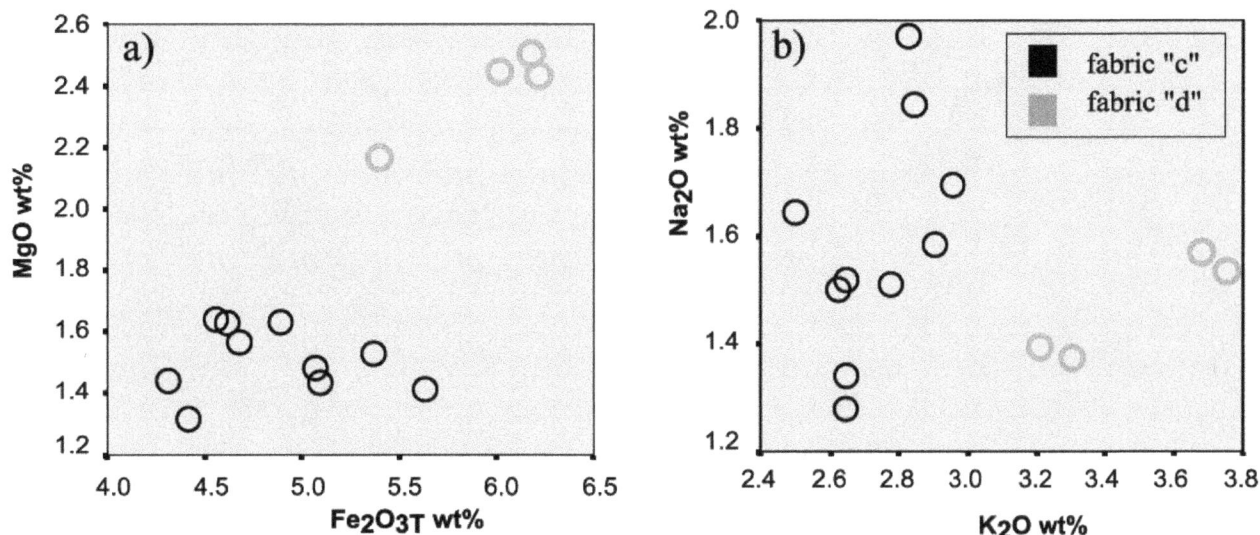

Fig. 4.3: Bivariate plots of the chemical compositions of the tiles produced by the Cohorts. The compositions split into two groups according to the petrographic observations.

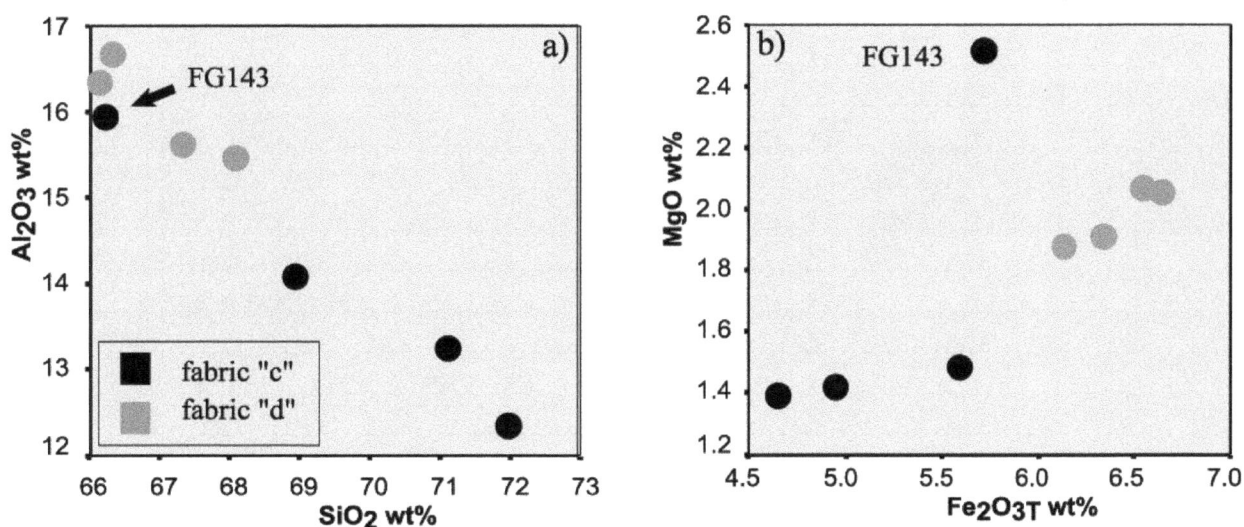

Fig. 4.4: Compositional diagrams of the analysed antefixa (frontal tiles). Two chemical groups seem to be present and to correspond, to the petrographic fabrics. Only sample FG143 has a chemical composition that does not corresponds to those of the other antefixa with petrographic fabric "d"

4.2 The production of the two legions

In the previous paragraph, the whole tile production at Vindonissa was examined. In Fig 4.5 the compositions of tiles produced by the two legions are compared and plotted in function of their archeological site of provenance. It is important to notice that there is not a correlation between the provenance of the object and its chemical signature. It is also evident that the tiles of the 11st legion have a more uniform composition, compared to those of the 21st legion. The concentrations of SiO_2 and Al_2O_3 vary only by 15 and 10 wt% respectively, which is significantly lower than the variations recorded for the 21st legion production. It is not possible for tiles of the 11th legion to define an internal structure in the data set and to discriminate the objects based on their stamp types. All but one sample (FG58), plot in elliptical clouds of points, displaying good correlation trends between different major elements (fig.4.5). The unusual composition of sample FG58 is due to a very

inhomogeneous fabric, characterised by the presence of large silt and greywacke rock fragments.

4.3 Other tile productions

One aim of this work was to compare the "Vindonissa tiles" to other military tile productions, specially the productions of the 21st and 11th legions related to other military posts (Strasbourg and Rottweil). Fig. 4.6 reports the chemical compositions of ceramics of different provenance: analyses from Vindonissa, Strasbourg, *Augusta Rauricorum* (Maggetti and Galetti, 1994), Rottweil (Schneider and Sommer, 2001) and Mainz (Dolata, 2000). The three tiles from Strasbourg are rather well distinguishable from the Swiss ones based on their major and trace elements compositions. Although these samples plot always near the scatter of points formed by the tiles from Vindonissa, they are never comparable to any of the defined chemical groups. For these samples, it was possible to compare only chemical composition since

21

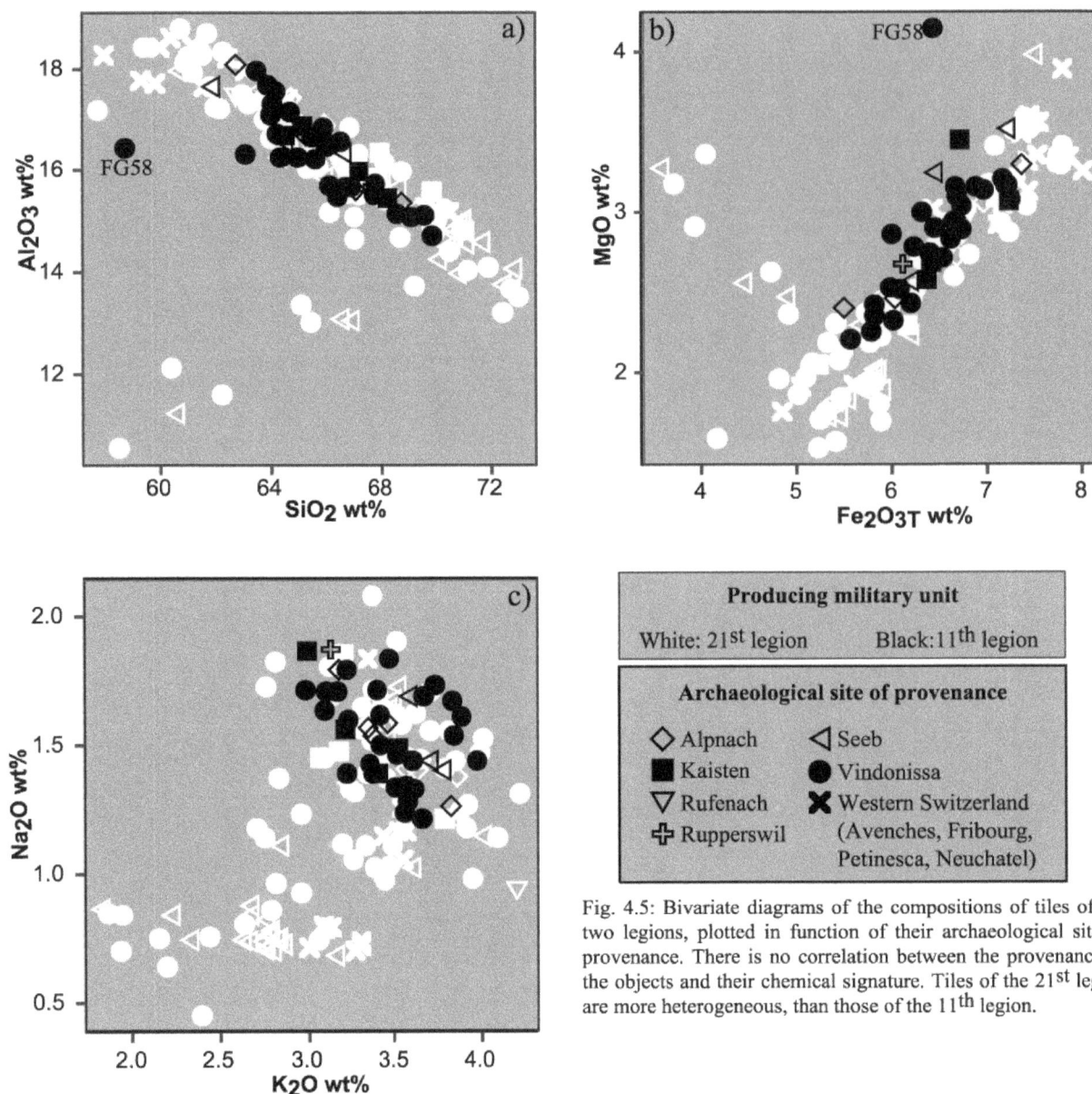

Fig. 4.5: Bivariate diagrams of the compositions of tiles of the two legions, plotted in function of their archaeological site of provenance. There is no correlation between the provenance of the objects and their chemical signature. Tiles of the 21st legion are more heterogeneous, than those of the 11th legion.

the specimens were too small to obtain a petrographic thin section. The two unstamped samples from Vindonissa are similar to the whole Vindonissa production, although some trace elements such as Sr and Rb display important variations. Vindonissa tiles differ also markedly from the tiles of the 21st legion found in Mainz (Dolata, 2000) and of the 11th legion found in Rottweil (Schneider and Sommer, 2001). Finally, the production of the 1st legion *Martiorum* (Maggetti and Galetti, 1994), which was garrisoned at *Augusta Rauricorum* is not comparable to any of the previously mentioned groups of tiles.

The data from Vindonissa and Strasbourg as well as those from *Augusta Rauricorum* (Maggetti and Galetti, 1994) are displayed in figure 4.6 without the loss on ignition (L.O.I.) recalculation. This, was made to reconcile all the data, since for those of Dolata (2000) and of Schneider and Sommer (2001) the L.O.I. values were not available.

4.4 The pottery of the 11th legion

12 pot-sherds from Vindonissa and 5 from Rottweil were analysed. The two groups of samples are chemically not comparable. This is not surprising, since the ceramic bodies are also different (see also section 3.2), this suggesting the use of different raw materials. The pots from Vindonissa made by the 11th legion are quite different in composition from the Rottweil pottery as well as from the tiles of the same legion. Compared to the tiles, Vindonissa pots have commonly higher concentrations in SiO_2, CaO and lower amounts of MgO, Na_2O and K_2O. In figure 4.7 the chemical data for these samples are compared to the tiles of the legion Claudia and to the compositional field of the tiles with fabric "c" and "a". Except sample FG217, which has a peculiar chemical composition, a partial compositional overlap can be noticed between fabric "c" and "a" tiles and the pottery of the 11th legion from Vindonissa.

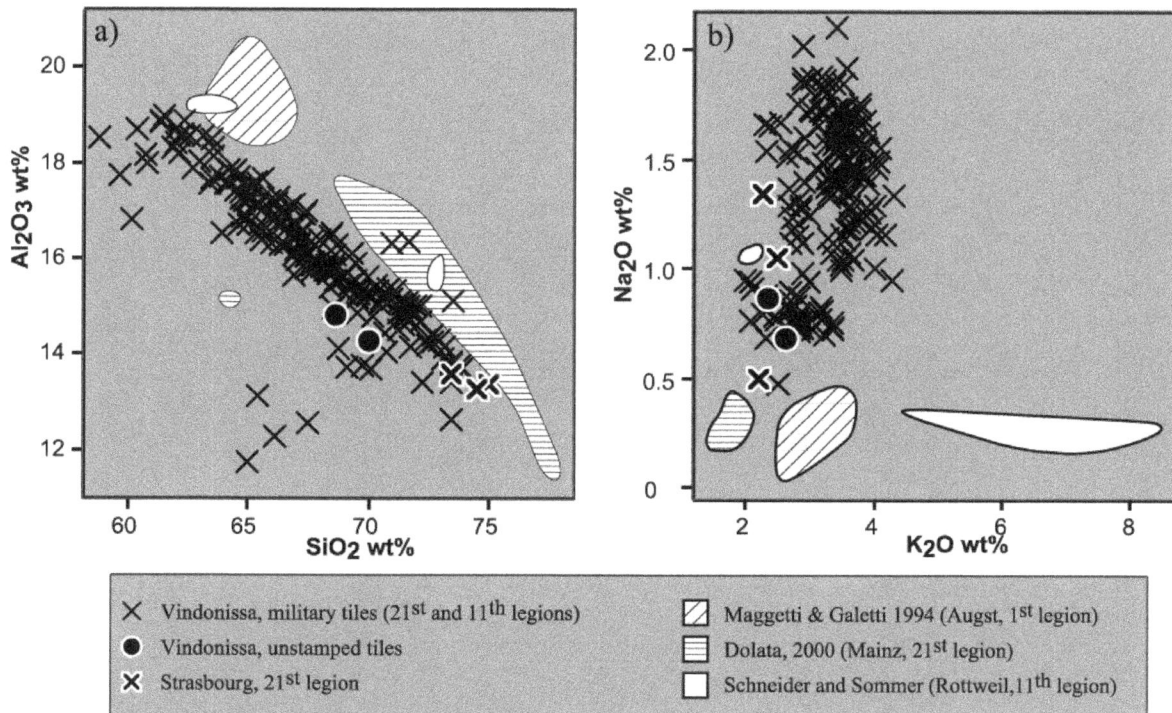

Fig. 4.6: Chemical plots reporting the compositions of different productions from the literature, compared to the tiles from Vindonissa and to the three tiles from Strasbourg.

4.5 The chemical and petrographic groupings and the unclassified samples

The Vindonissa tiles do not show any correlation between their archaeological site of finding and their chemical composition. Five major chemical groups arise from the observation of the bi-variate plots. Three of them correspond well to the petrographic fabrics "a", "b" and "c". The other two groups consist of the tiles of the petrographic fabric "d". The smallest group is composed of 13 tiles with stamp type 4 (L·XXIC·), whereas the largest group consists of the "Rupperswil tiles" and the rest of tiles with stamp type 4. Although there is commonly good accordance between petrographic fabric and chemical properties, various samples do not follow this strict subdivision, as shown in figures 4.1 to 4.5 in which some samples scatter from the defined chemo-petrographic groupings. Those tiles stamped L·XXIC· (type 4), which appear to be fairly similar to the "Rupperswil tiles", lie often in a marginal position of the scatter of point (fig. 4.2 a, b and c). Six additional Vindonissa stamped tiles of the 21st legion (FG10, FG56, FG60, FG97, FG115 and FG117), the three tiles from Strasbourg and the two unstamped tiles, are not classified in any of the chemo-petrographic groups. All the 6th cohort Raetorum production and four frontal tiles (FG126, FG133, FG135, FG143) do not match very well with any group of samples. Finally, the compositions of 11th legion's tiles are rather homogeneous and only one sample (FG58) appears to be different from all the others.

An attempt of classifying all these objects will be carried out in the next chapter by statistical analyses.

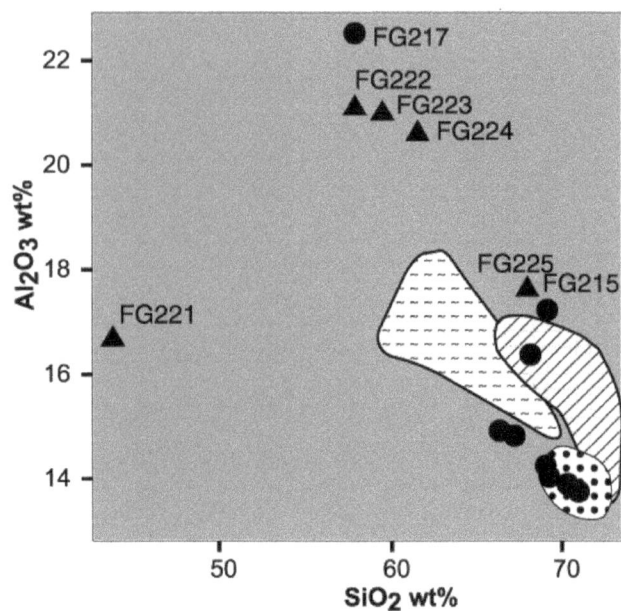

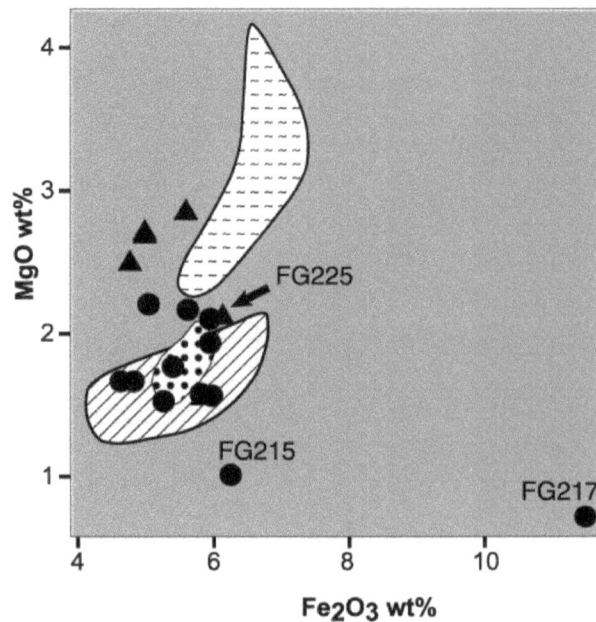

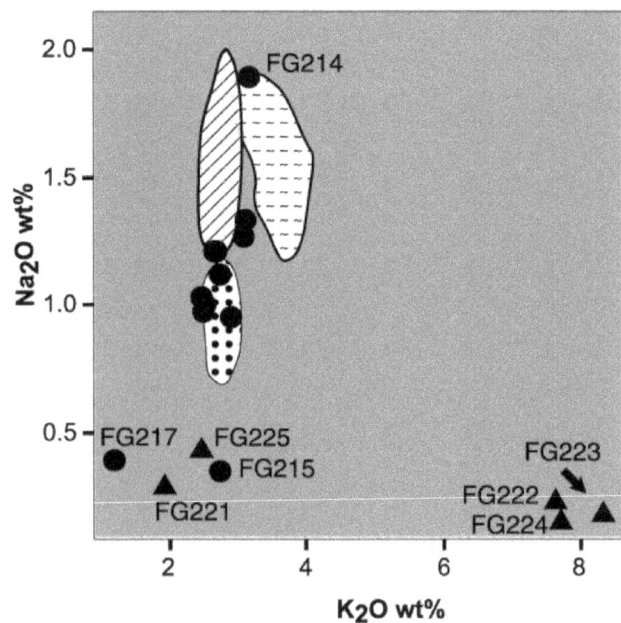

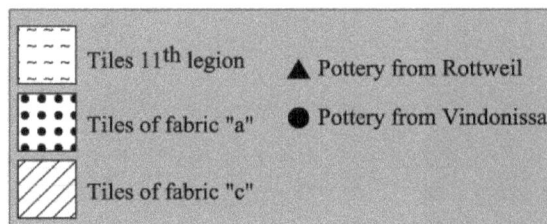

Fig. 4.7: The chemical composition of tiles and pottery of the 11th legion. The pottery from Rottweil and Vindonissa are easily distinguishable. Vindonissa pottery does not match the compositional field of the 11th legion's tiles, but is more similar totiles of fabric "a" and tiles of fabric "c".

5. Statistical data treatment

This chapter deals with the statistical analyses of chemical data as tool to classify the objects with indefinite petrochemical characteristics. Statistical terms like case, population and discriminant group will be used. A case is a single ceramic sample. The population is the ensemble of all cases considered in the statistical analyses. A discriminant group is a subset of cases with similar and homogeneous petro-chemical characteristics. The definition of discriminant groups is essential for the classification of cases with uncertain characteristics and for the definition of those cases, which are to be considered as unclassifiable or outliers. To define such groups, the petrographic fabrics, all bivariate chemical plots and the stamp-groupings were evaluated. Several

principal component analyses (PCA) were done with the entire population and data subsets, representing the various productions or specific assemblages of samples (stamped tiles, pottery and frontal tiles). In this way, it was possible to validate from a chemical point of view, the petrographic fabrics and to recognise the cases chemically not comparable to the mean composition of each group. In a first stage, all cases with ambiguous petrographic fabrics or with a chemical composition that did not match with the petrographic groups, were removed from the data set. With the remaining samples, discriminant groups for the successive discriminant analysis (DA) were built. These groups were formed by samples with very well characterised petrographic fabric and chemical compositions. With the DA, I could attempt to attribute to one of the groups the cases with ambiguous characteristics. Finally, to find out about the raw

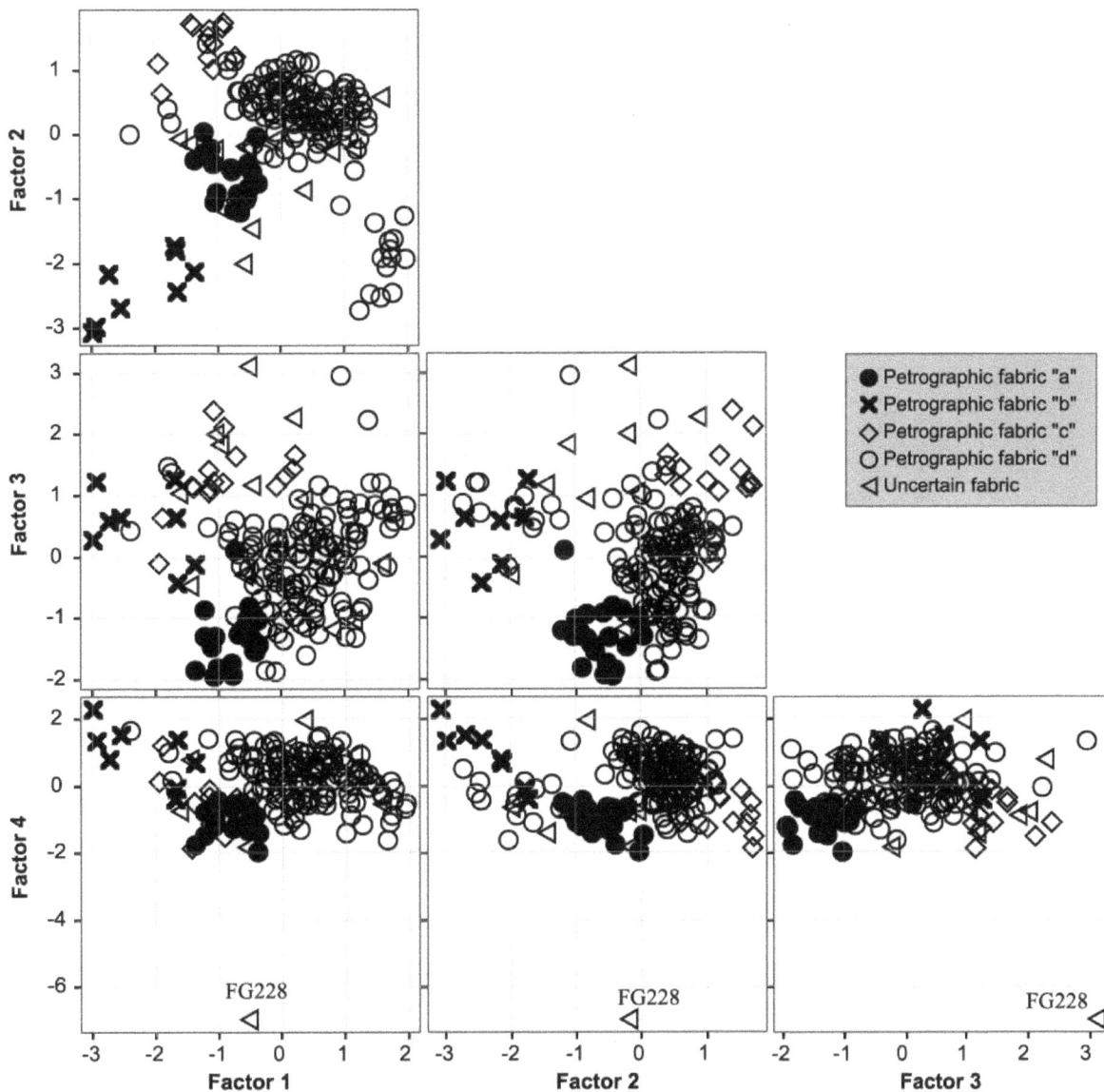

Fig. 5.1: Binary plots of the first four principal components extracted after PCA on all tile samples. Total variance explained by the first four components is 78.7% (186 cases).

materials used for the production of ceramics and tiles, local clays were attributed to predefined groups as discussed in the sixth chapter.

5.1 Principal component analysis

The petrographic observations and chemical results have demonstrated that the "Vindonissa tiles" are heterogeneous. Petrographic fabric and chemical signature are in most cases correlated whereas provenance of the objects and chemical signature are commonly uncorrelated. PCA with the entire population following the procedure explained in annexe B.4, was carried out to validate the petrographic and chemical observations. By creating two-dimensional plots of the first three to four components extracted, it was possible to obtain a representation of the sample distribution in a multidimensional space of chemical variables. As discussed in annexe B.4, the first three to four components always explain approximately 75-80% of the total variance in the populations, hence they are a good approximation of the real distribution of the samples in the multidimensional space.

The binary plots shown in figure 5.1 represent the result of the first PCA on all tile samples. Several groups are clearly defined in the data set and are generally in good accordance with the petrographic fabrics. Sample FG228, appears completely different from the average composition of other tiles. The picture, however, is still confusing because of the large number of cases considered.

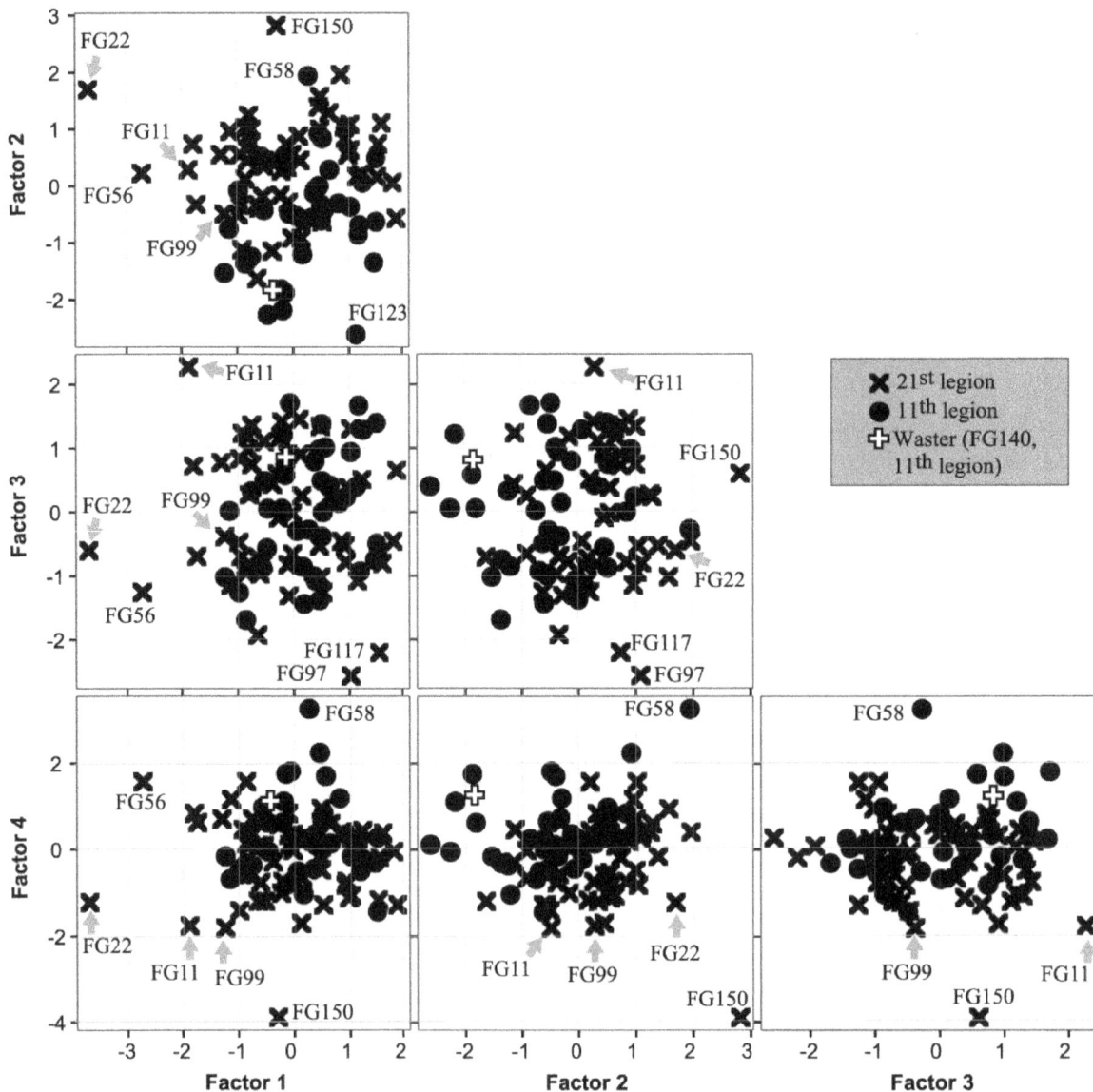

Fig. 5.2: Binary plots of the first four principal components for the "Rupperswil tiles" (stamp types 1,2,3,9,11,14,15 and 16). The composition of the waster (FG140) corresponds rather well to the average composition of the whole group. Total variance explained by the first four components is 75.5% (95 cases).

Figure 5.2 is a plot of the first four components extracted after a PCA on the "Rupperswil tiles" only. There is a very good chemical correspondence between the tiles of the two legions, that are supposed to be produced in Rupperswil (Arnold, 1969; Fellmann, 1988). The white cross represents the waster (FG140, 11th legion's tile, stamp 16): as we can expect, this sample has a composition, which fits well into the group of samples bearing one of the Rupperswil stamps. Few cases split from the main point scatter. Three of them belong to the petrographic fabric "c" (grey arrows) whereas the other different cases commonly belong to the tiles with unclassified petrographic fabric (see also table 3.2). This confirms that the fabric plays an important role to determine the chemical composition of the samples.

After PCA, the discriminant groups were built by taking carefully into account all the data, which could help to define the ceramic provenance. All the tiles with uncertain petrographic fabric (table 3.2) were not considered in the construction of the discriminant groups. Moreover, the samples for which we found an important discrepancy between archaeological data and chemical/or petrographic compositions, were not considered in the construction of the discriminant groups. This is the case of the tiles of the 6th cohort *Raetorum* and all the tiles with stamp type 4 (L·XXIC·) which have a chemical affinity with the "Rupperswil tiles": there are no archaeological evidence to link these samples to the "Rupperswil tiles", but their chemical composition and petrographic fabric is rather similar (see figures 4.1 and 4.2). Finally, the eight tiles of petrographic fabric "b", despite their very peculiar petrographic, were not considered a discriminant group, because of the limited number of samples and of the heterogeneous chemical composition of the group.

Four groups (137 cases in total) were finally selected and used as starting point for the analysis and the attribution of the uncertain cases (all the remnant tiles). A notation relating to the petrographic fabric of the objects was used to unify the names of the discriminant groups:

1.   "Discriminant group A" is composed of 22 tiles of the 21st legion and includes the majority of tiles with petrographic fabric "a".

2.   "Discriminant group C" is composed by petrographic fabric "c" tiles (17 samples); it includes the majority of the cohorts production, four frontal tiles and three tiles of the 21st legion (FG11, FG22, FG99).

3.   "Discriminant group D1" is the largest group, composed by tiles with petrographic fabric "d" and it includes nearly all the "Rupperswil tiles" (85 samples).

4.   "Discriminant group D2" is constituted by only 13 tiles of fabric "d" with stamp L·XXIC·. As previously discussed (chapter 3), these tiles show a common petrographic fabric (fabric "d"), but a very particular chemical signature (paragraph 4.1). Thus they cannot be considered equal to the other tiles with petrographic fabric "d". Because of these chemical differences, but also archaeological evidences (stamp type, geographical distribution of the finds), the samples of petrographic fabric "d" were divided into the two subgroups "D1" and "D2" ignoring the petrographic similarities.

Table 5.1 reports the samples chosen to build the four discriminant groups. All the cases not selected for the discriminant groups will be considered as unclassified: the scope of the discriminant analysis will be to attempt to attribute them to one of the discriminant groups.

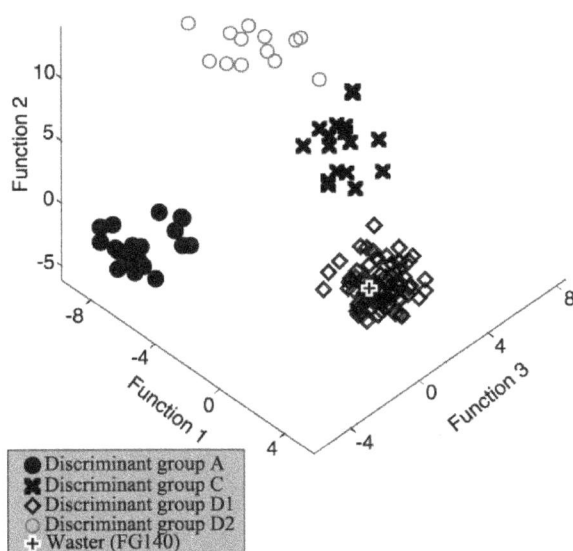

Fig. 5.3: Three-dimensional diagram showing the distribution of the four discriminant groups in the space defined by the discriminant functions. Each group is well characterised.

5.2 The attribution of unclassified cases by DA

To check the validity of the groups, I ran the first discriminant analysis on the selected 137 samples that form the four discriminant groups. The analysis correctly attributed each case to the expected group. Moreover, to check the validity of the attribution, two samples from each group were randomly selected and put in one of the other three groups. The subsequent DA was able to recognise all the "masked" samples and to correctly attribute them.

Figure 5.3 shows the results of the first DA. The histograms in fig. 5.4 represent the squared Mahalanobis' distances (D^2) of all cases from the four group centroids. The groups A, C, D1 and D2 are very well characterised in the space defined by the three discriminant functions. Actually, the maximum D^2 within groups is always less than 17, whereas the minimum D^2 between groups is greater than 54 for the two closest groups.

The following step was to include in the discriminant analysis all the samples (60) that were considered unclassified and to test their possible belonging to one group. This number includes also the 17 analysed legionary pots. For a limited number of cases with peculiar characteristics petrographic and chemical data allowed to exclude the assignment to one of the groups. This is the case for the three tiles from Strasbourg (FG226-FG228), the two unstamped tiles from Vindonissa (FG141 and FG142) and the five legionary-pots from Rottweil (FG221-FG225). For the other cases it was necessary to resort to discriminant analysis to check whether they belonged to a group or they had to be considered outliers. Table 5.2 reports the unclassified cases and their tentative assignment following archaeological data and petrographic and chemical characteristics. The last column represents the predicted attribution to one of the discriminant groups after statistical data treatment. Figure 5.5a/h shows the squared Mahalanobis distances (D^2) of the unclassified cases with respect to the closest group.

- Unclassified stamp type 4 (L·XXIC·) tiles

Fig. 5.5a shows that 12 of the 19 unclassified tiles with stamp type 4 (L·XXIC·) fall within the range of the D^2 for the cases belonging to the discriminant group D1, therefore they can be considered to belong it. Of the remaining seven cases, five (FG47, FG147, FG155,FG160, FG197) are close to the group ($16<D^2<21$) and most likely fit in it, whereas two (FG145 and FG151) have $D^2 >29$ and can not be attributed to this group.

- Unclassified "Rupperswil tiles"

Fig. 5.5 b to e report the results of DA of six unclassified tiles with "Rupperswil stamps". Samples FG56, FG97, FG117 can be clearly attributed to discriminant group D1, as their D^2 is always inside the range of the D^2 for this group (fig. 5.5b). Sample FG10 has the same D^2 from two discriminant groups (D1 and C) and can therefore not be attributed to either of the two (fig. 5.5b/c). Sample FG150 behaves clearly as an outlier, with $D^2=166$ from the nearest group centroid (discriminant group C), as shown in fig.5.5c. The behaviour of this sample may be explained by the fact that the object is probably

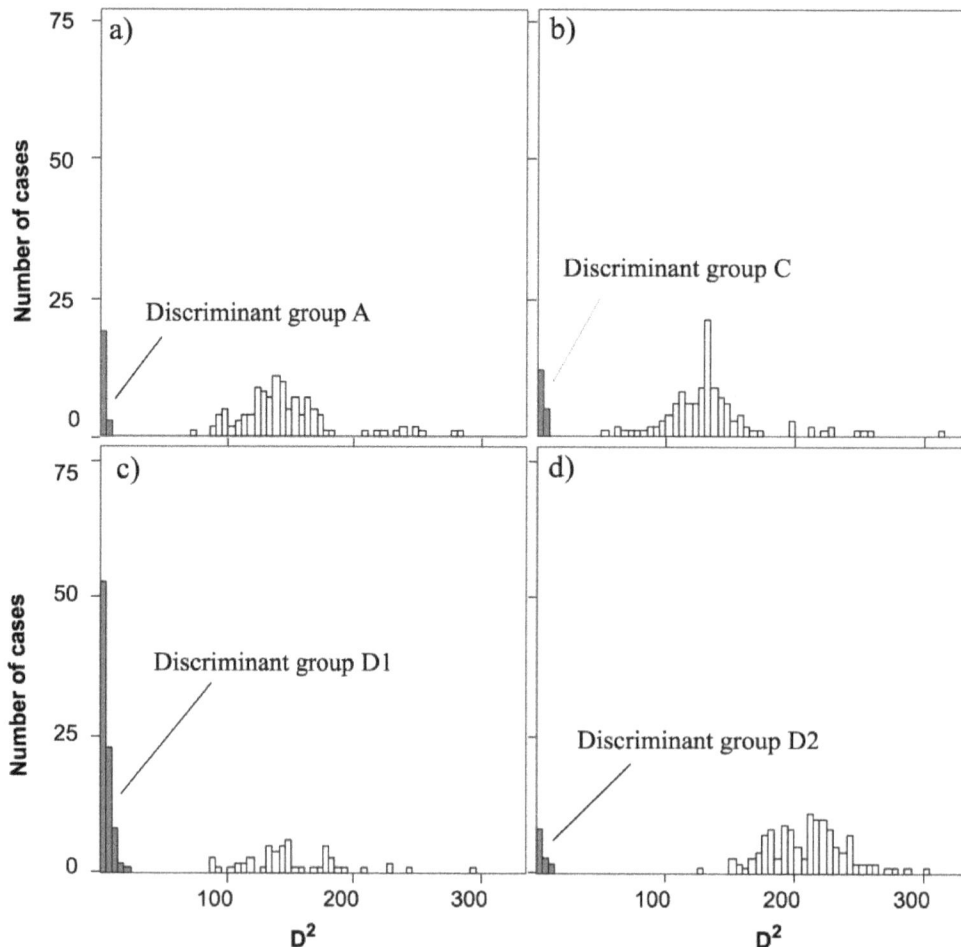

Fig. 5.4: histograms of the D^2 for all cases from the four group centroids, showing that the discriminant groups do not overlap among themselves.

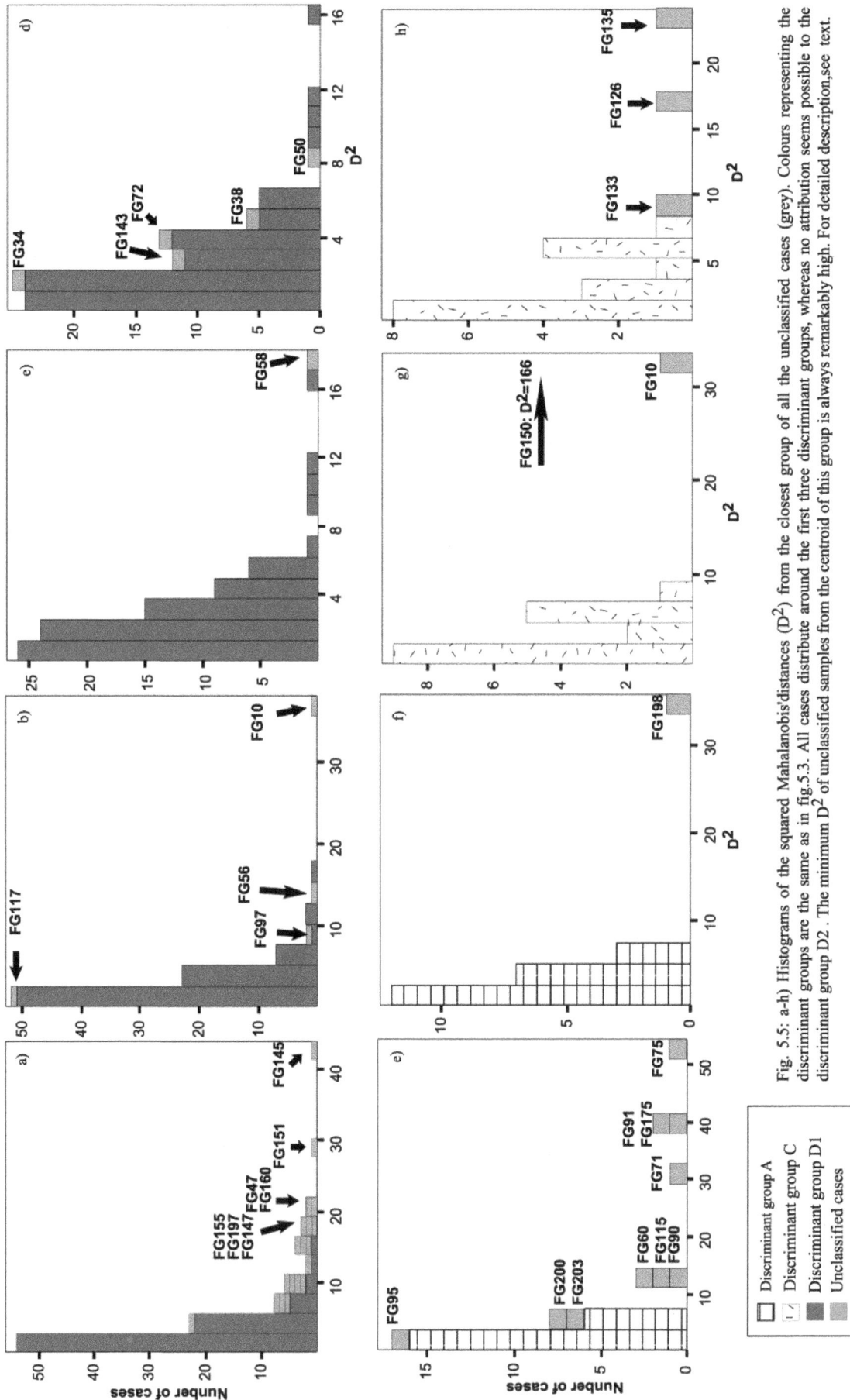

Fig. 5.5: a-h) Histograms of the squared Mahalanobis'distances (D^2) from the closest group of all the unclassified cases (grey). Colours representing the discriminant groups are the same as in fig.5.3. All cases distribute around the first three discriminant groups, whereas no attribution seems possible to the discriminant group D1. The minimum D^2 of unclassified samples from the centroid of this group is always remarkably high. For detailed description,see text.

☐ Discriminant group A
☒ Discriminant group C
■ Discriminant group D1
▨ Unclassified cases

Discriminant group	Number of cases	Sample ID
Discriminant group A	22	FG23, FG24, FG25, FG33, FG36, FG74, FG96, FG174, FG176, FG177, FG178, FG179, FG180, FG181, FG182, FG196, FG201, FG202, FG204, FG205, FG206, FG207
Discriminant group C	17	FG11, FG22, FG35, FG37, FG39, FG40, FG57, FG59, FG61, FG77, FG98, FG99, FG110, FG130, FG131, FG132, FG134
Discriminant group D1	85	FG12, FG13, FG14, FG15, FG20, FG21, FG26, FG27, FG28, FG29, FG30, FG31, FG32, FG41, FG51, FG52, FG53, FG54, FG55, FG62, FG63, FG64, FG65, FG66, FG67, FG68, FG69, FG70, FG73, FG76, FG78, FG79, FG80, FG81, FG84, FG87, FG88, FG89, FG92, FG93, FG94, FG100, FG101, FG102, FG103, FG104, FG107, FG108, FG109, FG111, FG112, FG113, FG114, FG116, FG118, FG119, FG120, FG121, FG122, FG123, FG140, FG161, FG163, FG164, FG165, FG166, FG167, FG168, FG169, FG170, FG171, FG172, FG173, FG183, FG184, FG185, FG186, FG187, FG188, FG189, FG191, FG193, FG194, FG195, FG199
Discriminant group D2	13	FG16, FG17, FG18, FG19, FG48, FG146, FG149, FG152, FG153, FG154, FG158, FG159, FG190

Table 5.1: Sample list and number of cases for the four established discriminant group (137 cases in total).

contaminated during burial (P_2O_5 = 0.56wt% and Ba=690 ppm).

Sample FG198, with a $D^2>35$ from the centroid of discriminant group A, cannot be attributed to this group with certainty (fig.5.5d). Finally, fig 5.5e reports the result for the only tile of the legion 11th production, which remained unclassified due to its petrographic texture (FG58). The D^2 plot shows that there is a certain probability that it belongs to the discriminant group D1, as its D^2 is only slightly greater than the maximum D^2 for this group.

- Unclassified tiles with stamp types 12 and 13 (21st legion)

All tiles with stamp type 13 (petrographic fabric "b") were considered unclassified, together with sample FG60 (stamp type 12, L·XXI·L) and FG115 (uncertain stamp type 12 or 13?). Figure 5.5f displays the results after DA on these samples. There is only a partial superposition of tiles with stamp type 13 with the discriminant group A. The cases matching best (FG95, FG200, FG203), as shown by the petrographic investigations, are those poorer in the calcareous clay component. Samples FG60, FG90 and FG115 are near the group and probably belong to it. In contrast, the remaining tiles with stamp 13 are more distant ($D^2>29$). The ceramic body of these samples actually contains a high percentage of calcareous clay.

- Unclassified Cohort- and frontal tiles

Figure 5.5g and 5.5h show that the unclassified Cohorts and frontal tile-samples split into two possible discriminant groups. All the tiles of the 6th cohort production and one frontal tile (FG143) are attributed to

the discriminant group D1. The petrographic analyses for these samples showed that their fabric was very similar to the fabric "d". The remaining three frontal tiles (FG126, FG133, FG135) are comparable to the composition of the discriminant group C, although not identical with D^2 ranging between 9 and 25 (fig. 5.5h). The attribution of these samples remains uncertain, since they could not clearly be classified into the petrographic fabric "c" because of the nearly absolute lack of the dark-brown ARFs characterising this type of fabric.

- Legionary pots

The pottery from Vindonissa has quite variable compositions but discriminant analysis pointed out a resemblance among the majority of the pottery and the discriminant groups A and C. Two samples (FG215, FG217) could not be attributed. In contrast, statistics attribute sample FG214 to the group D1. Table 5.2 summarises the results on Vindonissa pottery after discriminant analysis.

5.3 Limits of the technique

The used techniques are not free from limitations. One assumption that is made for the application of Discriminant Analysis is that the groups have multivariate normal distribution. This was true for the majority of the cases, although some variables (CaO and Sr) displayed a not perfect bell-shaped distribution, even after the standardisation (see Annexe B4).

The second problem is relative to the sample size. Statisticians (see Harbottle, 1976 cited in Baxter 1994) suggest that to perform safe attribution with a linear Discriminant Analysis, the ratio n/p between the number of observations (n) and the number of variables (p) should be greater than 3. This is the case just for one the discriminant group D1, whereas all the others are relatively small.

This is always a major problem when dealing with archaological objects, since the availability of samples is commonly not infinite. For this reason, the interpretation of statistical data should not be taken as an absolute truth, but as a tool to help and improve the archaeological interpretations.

Sample	Stamp type	Object	Fabric	DA attribution
FG10	Stamps Rupp.	21st tile	d?	not attributed
FG34	5	cohorts' tile	d	Group D1
FG38	5	cohorts' tile	d	Group D1
FG47	4	21st tile	d	Group D1?
FG49	4	21st tile	d	Group D1
FG50	5	cohorts' tile	d	Group D1
FG56	Stamps Rupp.	21st tile	a?	Group D1
FG58	Stamps Rupp.	11th tile	?	Group D1?
FG60	12	21st tile	a-b?	Group A?
FG71	13	21st tile	b	not attributed
FG72	5	cohorts' tile	d	Group D1
FG75	13	21st tile	b	not attributed
FG82	4	21st tile	d	Group D1
FG83	4	21st tile	d	Group D1
FG85	4	21st tile	d	Group D1
FG86	4	21st tile	d	Group D1
FG90	13	21st tile	b	Group A?
FG91	13	21st tile	b	not attributed
FG95	13	21st tile	b	Group A
FG97	Stamps Rupp.	21st tile	?	Group D1
FG105	4	21st tile	d	Group D1
FG106	4	21st tile	d	Group D1
FG115	12-13?	21st tile	a-b?	Group A?
FG117	Stamps Rupp.	11st tile	d?	Group D1
FG126	-	Frontal tile	d	not attributed
FG133*	-	Frontal tile	d	Group C?
FG135*	-	Frontal tile	d	not attributed
FG143	-	Frontal tile	d?	Group D1
FG144	4	21st tile	d	Group D1
FG145	4	21st tile	d	not attributed
FG147	4	21st tile	d	Group D1?
FG148	4	21st tile	d	Group D1
FG150*	Stamps Rupp.	21st tile	d?	not attributed
FG151	4	21st tile	d	not attributed
FG155*	4	21st tile	d	Group D1?
FG156	4	21st tile	d	Group D1
FG157	4	21st tile	d	Group D1
FG160	4	21st tile	d	Group D1?
FG162	4	21st tile	d	Group D1
FG175	13	21st tile	b	not attributed
FG197	4	21st tile	d	Group D1?
FG198	Stamps Rupp.	21st tile	d?	Group A?
FG200	13	21st tile	b	Group A
FG203	13	21st tile	b	Group A
FG208	-	Pot Vind.	a?	Group A
FG209	-	Pot Vind.	a?	Group C
FG210	-	Pot Vind.	a?	Group C
FG211	-	Pot Vind.	a?	Group C
FG212	-	Pot Vind.	a?	Group C
FG213	-	Pot Vind.	a?	Group A
FG214	-	Pot Vind.	a?	Group D1
FG215	-	Pot Vind.	a?	not attributed
FG216	-	Pot Vind.	a?	Group A
FG217*	-	Pot Vind.	a?	not attributed
FG218	-	Pot Vind.	a?	Group A
FG219	-	Pot Vind.	a?	Group C

Table 5.2: Attribution of the uncertainly classified samples after DA.
*, cases with P2O5>0.5% (chemical compositions recalculated as ex-
plained in the annexe B7)

31

6. Characterisation of the local clays and comparison with the ceramic products

The comparison between final products (ceramics) and possible raw materials (clays) is based on the hypothesis that the petrographic composition of clays was not changed by the craftmen with purification or tempering processes. The comparison with the local clays is essential to make hypotheses on the provenance of the objects, when the heterogeneity of the sample compositions suggests the presence of different production sites or the use of different of raw materials. The clay samples were collected near Windisch, Kölliken, Rupperswil, Kaisten and Seeb. These sampling sites were chosen following the hypothesis formulated in the archaeological literature about the location of the production sites for Vindonissa tiles.

6.1 Geological setting

The geology of the alluvial planes between Kölliken and Windisch is dominated by Pleistocene fluvio-glacial and löss sediments. The hills rising on the southern bank of the Aare river mainly consist of oligo-miocenic lower and upper molasse. To the south and south-east of Vindonissa the offshoots of the Jura chain (mainly limestones and marls) cross the Aare valley and disappear under the molasse sediments.

Table 6.1 and fig. 6.1 report the sampling localities and the geological formation to which each sample belongs. Two specimens were collected from the alteration products of the lower sweet-water molasse, whereas all the other samples are from the common outcrops of glacial and fluvial sediments of the alluvial planes.

6.2 Petrography and mineralogy of the local clays

Petrographic analyses on local clays were performed on fired clay briquettes (see annexe B.2). The observations demonstrate that all but one specimen (FG5) are quartz-rich, calcareous poor sediments, characterised by a prevalence of the silt fraction over the clay fraction and by a variable non-plastic inclusion contents. Depending whether the texture is grain or mud supported, they may be classified as packstones or wackestones (Adams et al., 1988). The non-plastic grains are poorly sorted and cover a wide range of sizes from siltstone to coarse sandstone. They are generally angular to subangular and, following the classification of Pettijohn et al. (1987), the roundness index is between 0.2 and 0.3. Figure 6.2 shows photomicrographs of thin sections of representative fired clay briquettes. Mineralogical X-ray diffraction analyses showed that the clay fraction of all the samples is mainly composed of illite or illite and chlorite (fig. 6.3). The following paragraph describes shortly the petrography of the fired clays and classifies them into petrographic groups.

- FG1, FG2, FG3, FG42, FG43, FG45: These clays are grain-supported sediments (packstones). Their grain sizes ranges between silt and very fine sand. Grains with sand size are rare. Quartz predominates among the a-plastic inclusions; K-feldspar and Na-plagioclase are subordinate. Biotite, white mica flakes and epidote are accessories.

- FG46: this clay is a grain-supported sediment (packstone). The grain sizes range between a fine sandstone and a coarse silt, with non plastic inclusions of 0.05-0.25mm . Quartz and subordinate feldspars represent

Sample ID	Sampling site	Swiss coordinates	Geological formation / (depth in m)	Sample ID	Sampling site	Swiss coordinates	Geological formation / (depth in m)
FG1	Lupfig	657400/254800	Early to late Würmian sands and conglomerates / (1.5)	FG8	Kaisten	646075/265350	Late Würmian sands and conglomerates / (1)
FG2	Lupfig	657400/254800	Early to late Würmian sands and conglomerates / (2)	FG9	Kaisten	645825/264900	Late Würmian sands and conglomerates / (1)
FG3	Rupperswil	651837/249375	Glacial and late glacial muds / (1.5)	FG42	Rupperswil	650525/248662	Glacial muds (Glaziale Schwemmlehme) / (1)
FG4	Kölliken	645800/242100	Early to late Würmian sands and conglomerates / (1)	FG43	Rupperswil	652062/248300	Glacial and late glacial muds / (1)
FG5	Lupfig	657100/254225	Lower sweet water molasse / (2)	FG44	Seeb	680480/260070	Würmian moranes / (1)
FG6	Lupfig	657100/254225	Lower sweet water molasse / (1.5)	FG45	Hausen	658337/256475	Glacial and late glacial muds / (1)
				FG231	Seeb	680480/260070	Würmian moranes / (1.5)
FG7	Habsburg	656650/257125	Riss moranes / (1)	FG46	Rupperswil	651887/249200	Late Würmian sands and conglomerates / (1.5)

Table 6.1: Sampling locality, geographic coordinates and geological formation of the clay samples.

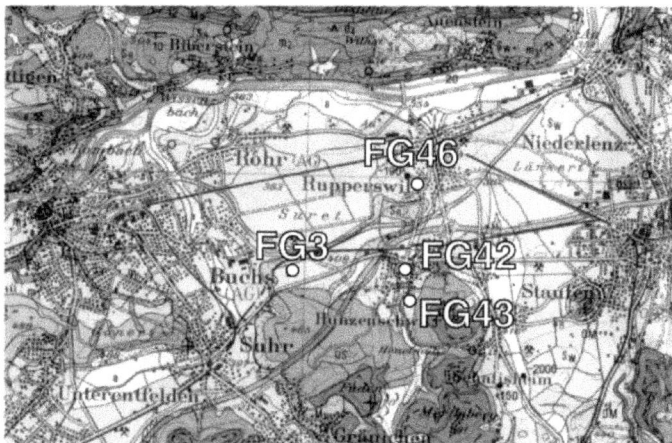

Fig. 6.1: Geological map of the main sampling areas. The sampling location for each specimen is indicated. Geological basis (scaled) from the Geologischen Karte der zentralen und Nordschweiz - 1:100000 (1984).

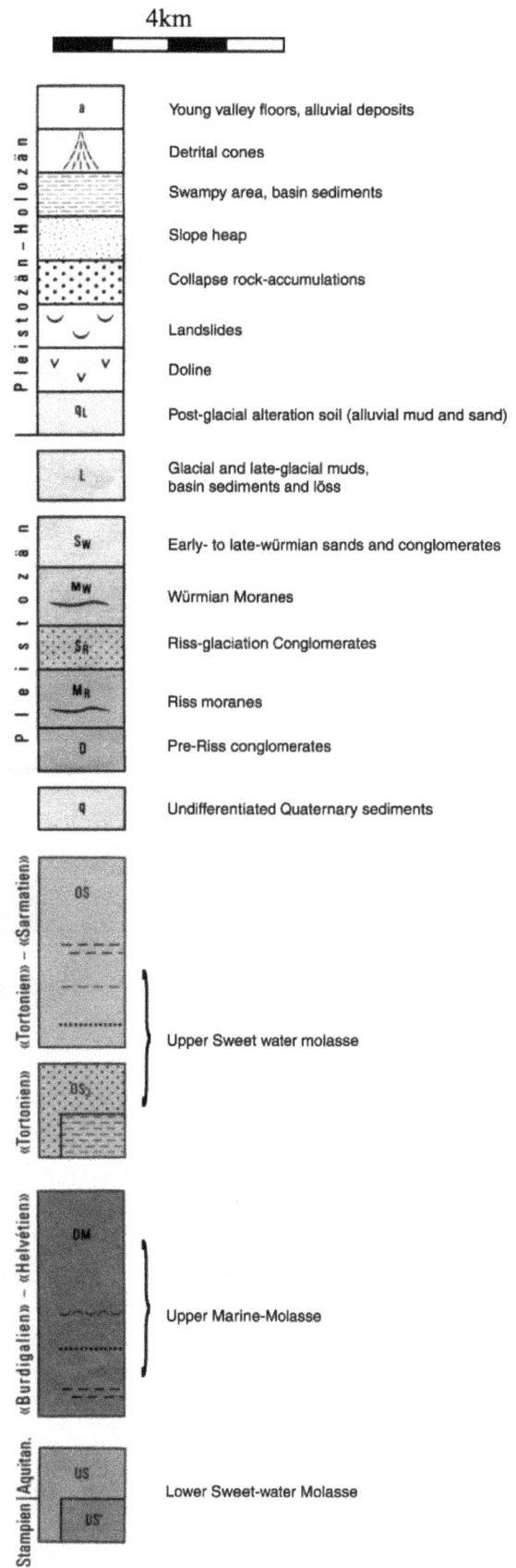

33

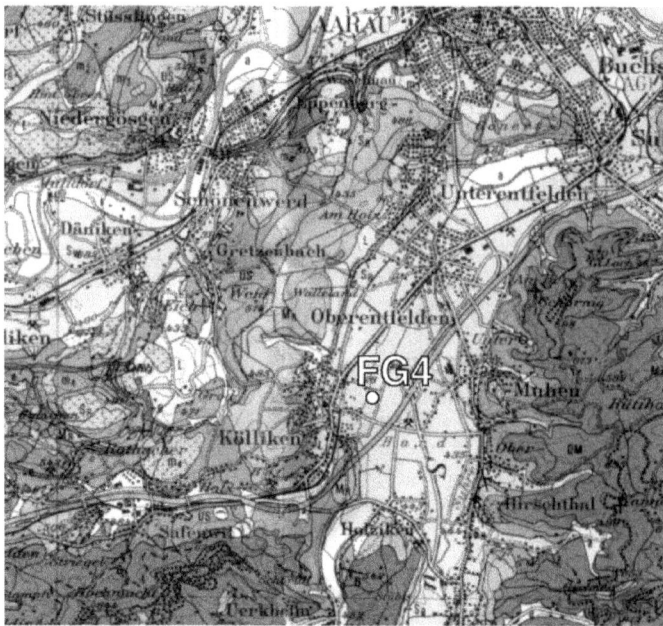

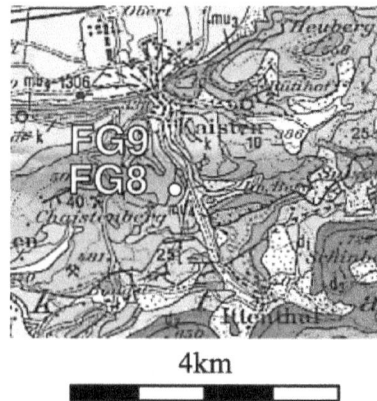

Fig. 6.1: continued, from the previous page.

the main constituents within the non plastic inclusions. Biotite and white micas are common accessories. Epidote is rare.

- FG4, FG7: the two samples are grain-supported sediments (packstones), the grain sizes range between a fine sandstone and a coarse silt. The clay sample FG7 has a slightly finer grain size than the sample FG4. Both samples are characterised by the presence of large dark-brown inclusions with a greywacke texture. Quartz and subordinate feldspars represent the main constituents of the grains. Biotite and white micas are common accessory phases.

- FG5, FG6: the two samples come from the same site. FG6 was deposited on the stratigraphic top of FG5.

The sample FG5 is a fine grained, grey marl with rare (less than 3 vol%) non plastic sand-sized inclusions. Quartz and feldspars fragments predominate over little limestone fragments. The clay matrix is fine grained, silt-poor and contains small (about 0.05 mm), dispersed biotite and white mica flakes and large crystals of brown amphibole.

- The clay FG6 is a fine-grained, clay-rich wackestone (matrix-supported texture). The grains display a serial distribution of sizes between 0.03 and 0.1 mm. Grains over 0.1 (up to 0.4 mm) are less frequent. Quartz, subordinate K-feldspar and Na-plagioclase represent nearly 100% of the non plastic inclusions.

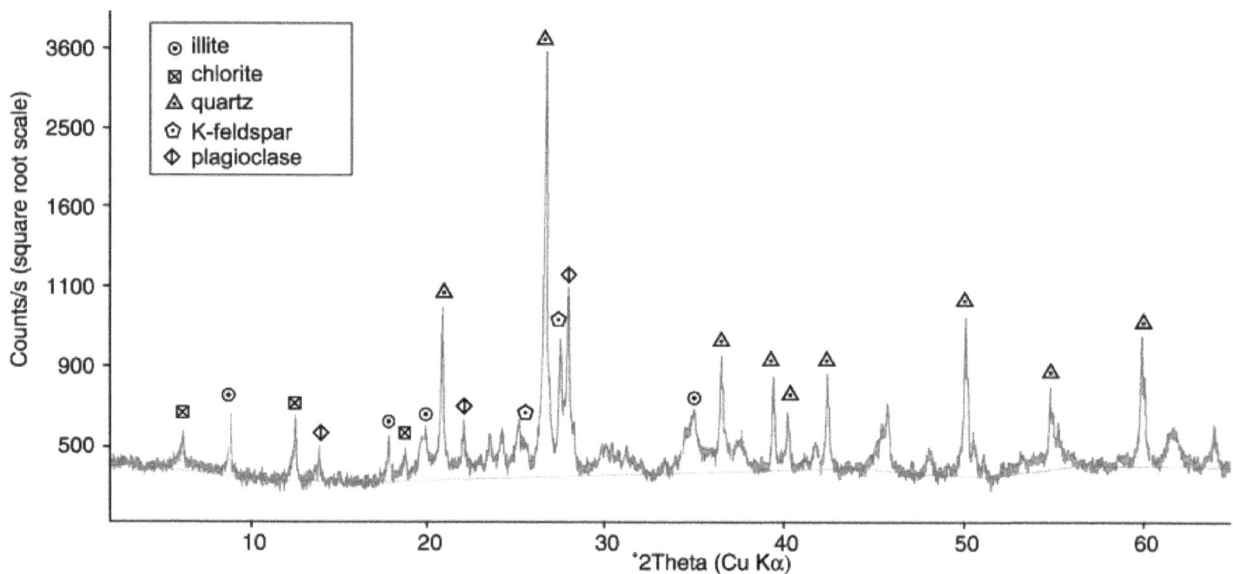

Fig. 6.3: Powder X-ray diffraction pattern of the clay sample FG46 (bulk analysis).The relative low intensity of the chlorite and illite peaks is due to the dilution effect by quartz and feldspar.

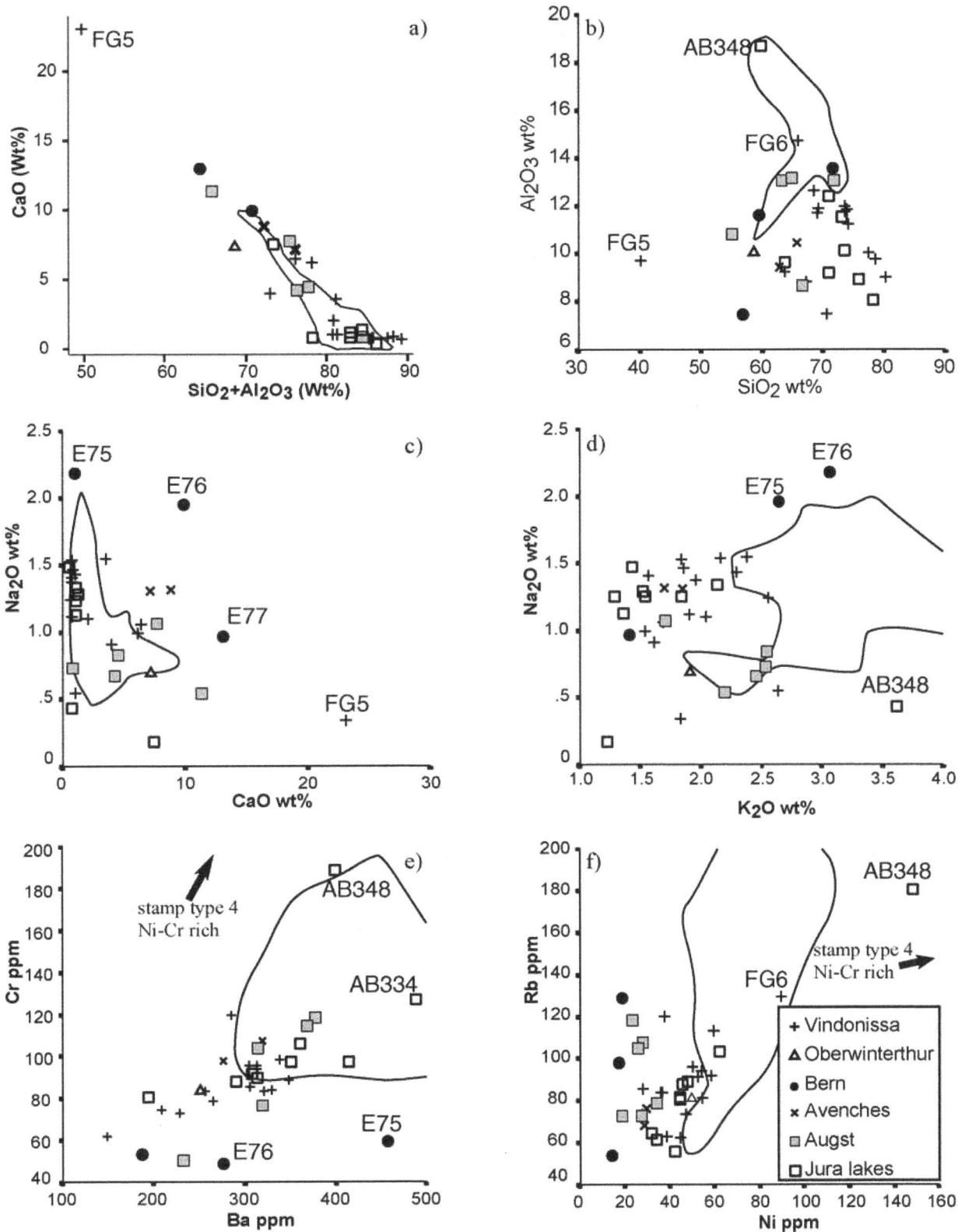

Fig. 6.4: Chemical composition of the 15 local clay samples and of the 18 samples from the literature. The compositional field of all Vindonissa stamped tiles is also reported. In e) and f) the field of Vindonissa tiles split into two groups because of the high Ni and Cr contents of the thirteen samples with stamp type 4 (see paragraph 4.1). This Ni-Cr rich subgroup plots outside the graphs e) and f).

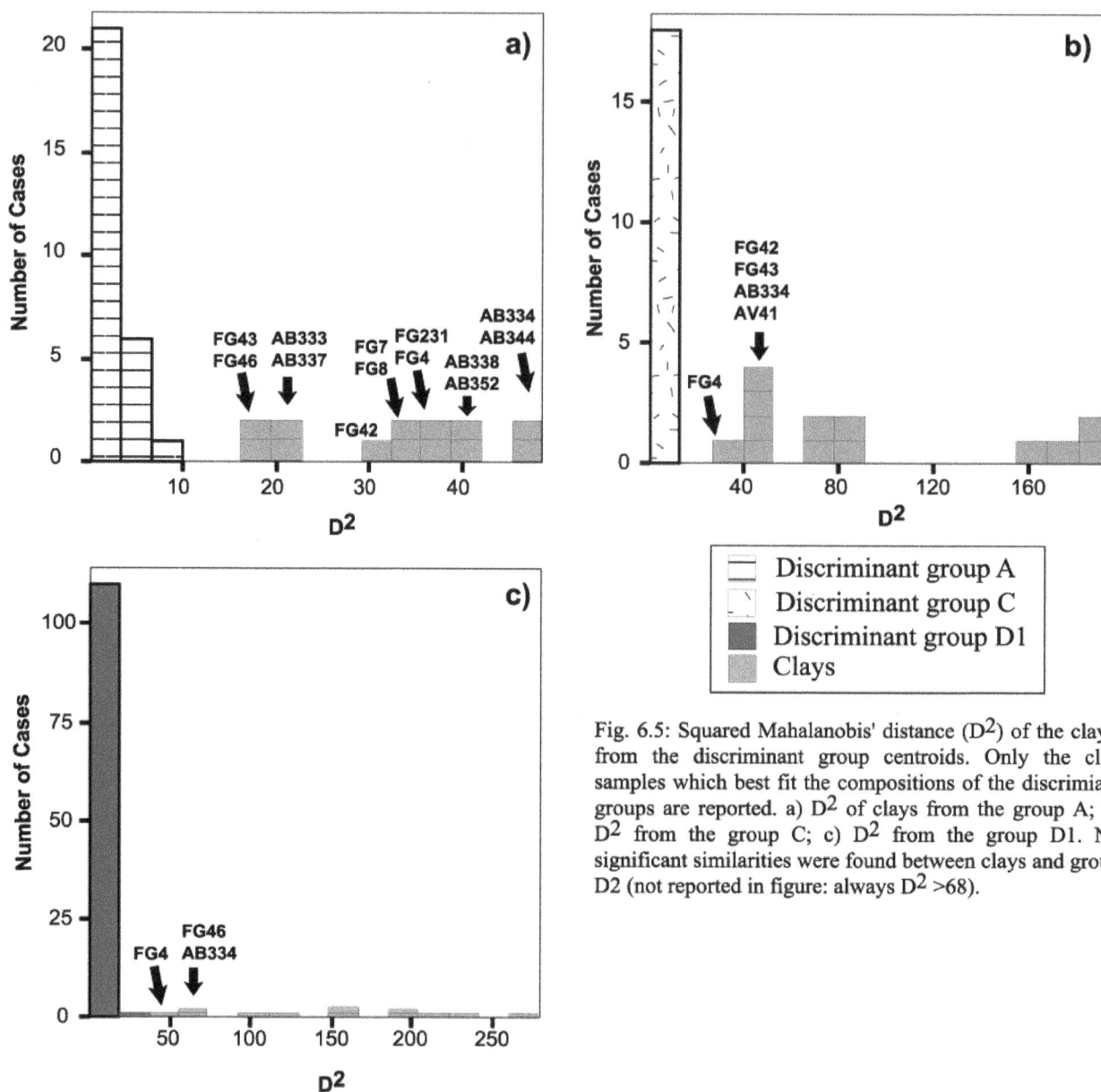

Fig. 6.5: Squared Mahalanobis' distance (D^2) of the clays, from the discriminant group centroids. Only the clay samples which best fit the compositions of the discrimiant groups are reported. a) D^2 of clays from the group A; b) D^2 from the group C; c) D^2 from the group D1. No significant similarities were found between clays and group D2 (not reported in figure: always $D^2 > 68$).

White mica flakes are accessory phases.

- FG8, FG9: fine grained wackestones. Non plastic inclusions display a wide range of grain sizes, from silt grains to grains larger than 2mm in diameter (micro-conglomerates). The latter are rare. They are principally composed of quartz, rounded limestone fragments, K -feldspar and white mica. Dark-brown clay pellets are occasionally present.

- FG44- FG231: these sand-rich packstones, are characterised by very angular grains. Non plastic inclusions are mainly composed of quartz and limestones fragments, with accessory feldspar grains.

6.3 Chemistry of the clays

To be able to localise the production sites of the ceramic bodies it was necessary to carry out chemical analyses of the local clay samples. In addition to the 15 sedimentary rocks that were sampled in the region, 18 published clay analyses were also considered. Table 6.2 summarises the details about these 18 additional samples (sampling site, reference). This set of analysed clays and published data covers a large area extending from the Swiss plateau to the Swiss plane and the Rhine valley. Despite the large region covered by the clay sampling, it is difficult to distinguish their provenance based on their chemistry only. As shown in fig. 6.4, the clays build a large scatter of point and their compositions range from Ca-poor (CaO < 2wt%) to Ca-rich (CaO up to 12wt%). Only a few samples have compositions, that lie clearly off the main point scatter. Samples FG5, FG6, AB348 and OW42 have peculiar characteristics, due to their different contents in Al_2O_3, SiO_2, CaO, MgO, Cr and Ni. Two samples from Bern (E75, E76) differ also from the main point scatter because of their slightly higher alkali contents. When compared to the composition of the investigated ceramic products (fig.6.4), the majority of

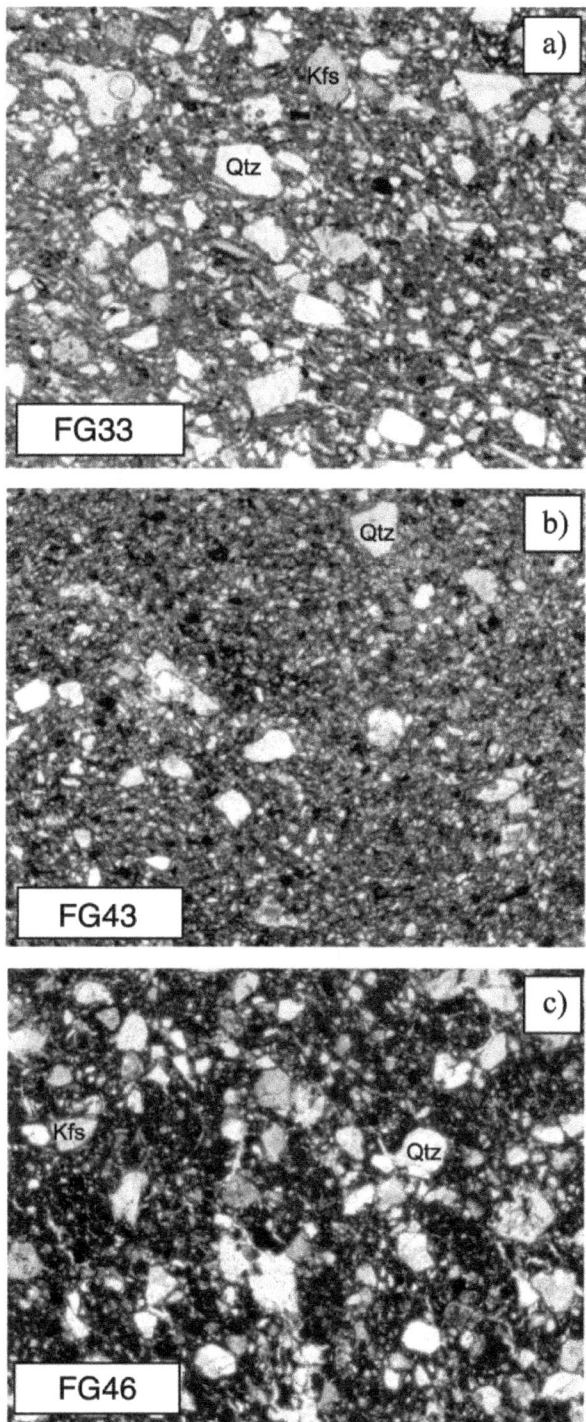

Fig. 6.6: Comparison between tiles and clays. a) One representative tile of group A (FG33) is compared to the clays FG43 (b) and FG46 (c), which are chemically the most similar ones, according to discriminant analysis. Petrographic investigations demonstrate that clay FG46 is the most likely raw material for group A, since it has also a similar texture . White rectangles are 1mm long.

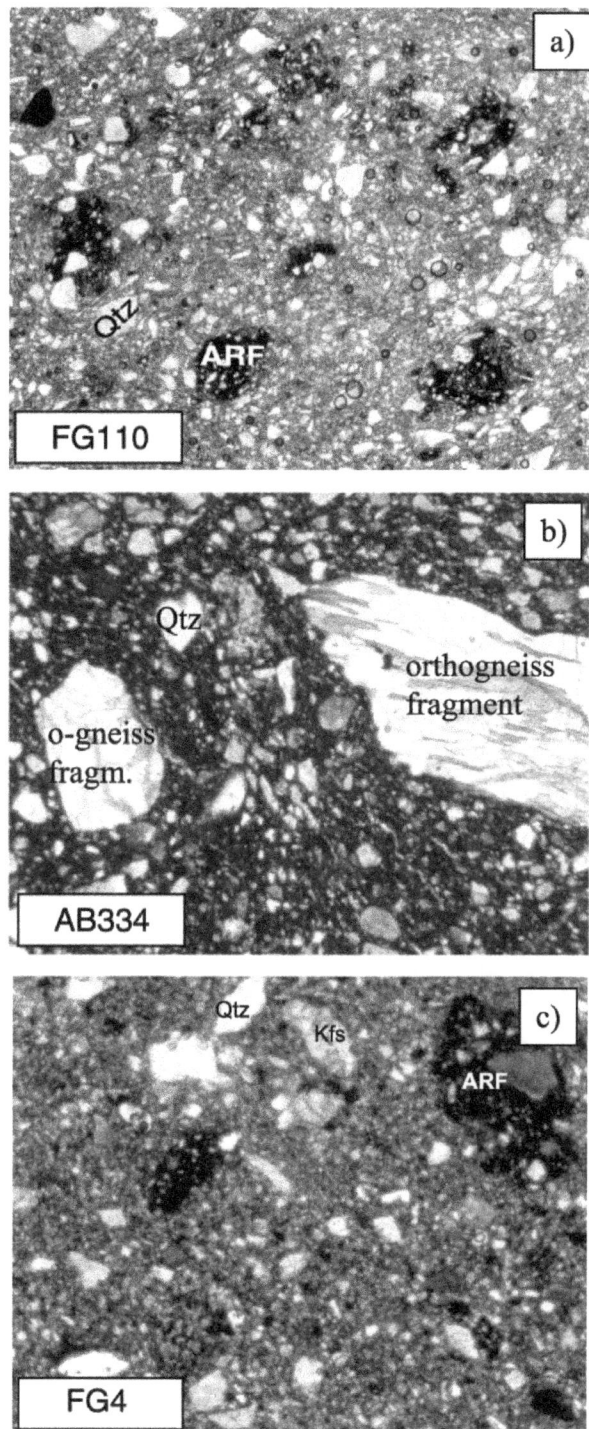

Fig. 6.7: Comparison between tile FG110, representative sample of the group C (a) and the two clays AB334 (b) and FG4 (c). Petrographic analysis helps to exclude that clay AB334 is a possible raw material for tiles of group C, even though the chemical compositions are rather similar. In constrast, clay FG4 is both petrographically and chemical similar to the tiles of group C. White rectangles are 1mm long.

the clays have higher SiO_2/Al_2O_3 ratios except samples FG6 and AB348. This is clearly a result of the quartz-rich nature of the sediments, which has been already discussed in the petrography section.

6.4 Clays and tiles: comparison by statistical data treatment

To outline the potential similarities between clays and ceramic products, statistical analyses comparing the clay composition to the four discriminant groups established

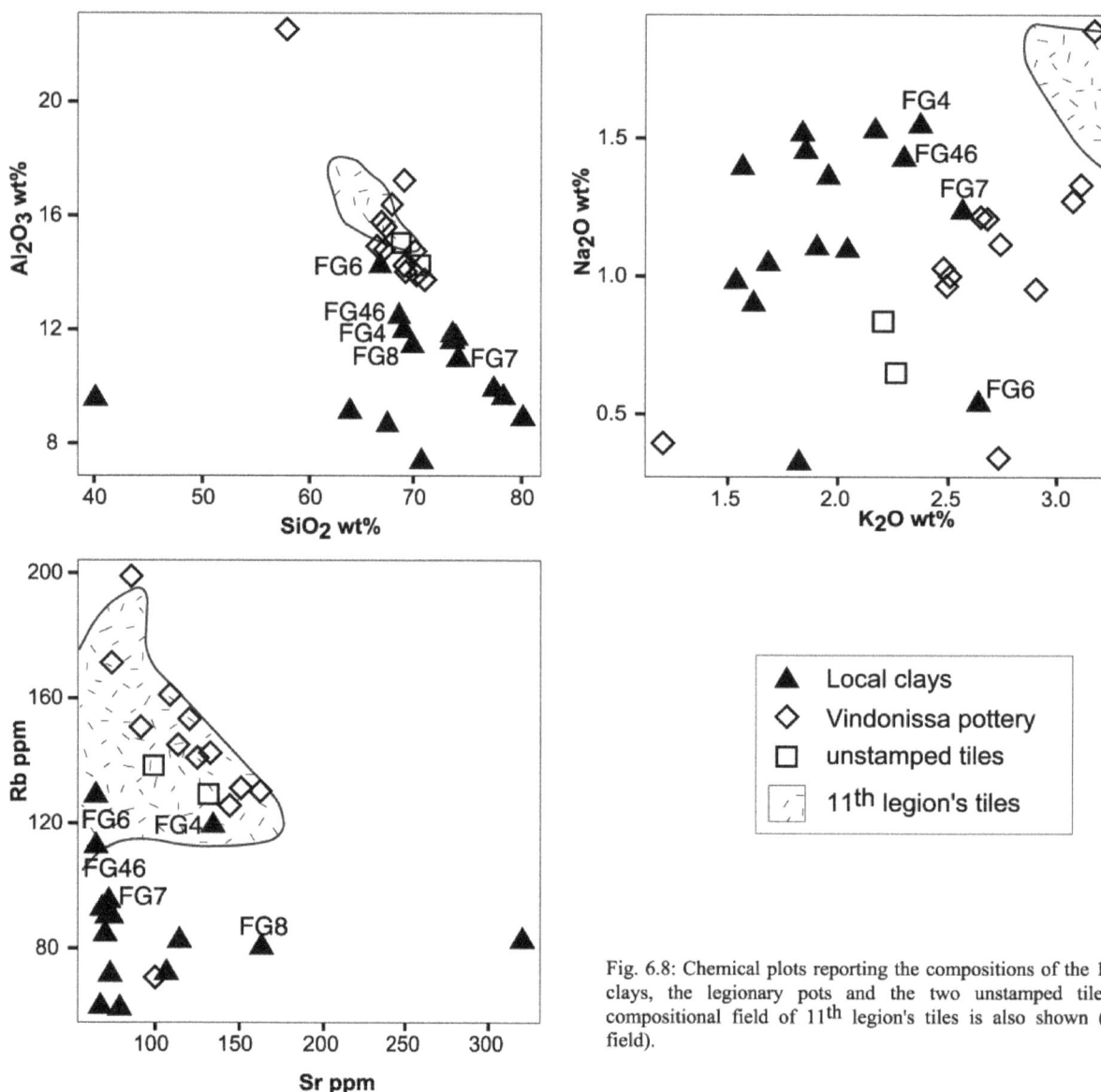

Fig. 6.8: Chemical plots reporting the compositions of the 15 local clays, the legionary pots and the two unstamped tiles. The compositional field of 11th legion's tiles is also shown (dashed field).

in section 5.2 were carried out. The selected clays were considered as unclassified objects. However, the analysis results were not completely satisfactory, since none of the samples perfectly matched the discriminant groups. Anyway, some interesting informations can be extracted from the Mahalanobis squared distances (D^2) between the clays and the centroids of the discriminant groups (fig. 6.5).

In the multivariate space of the chemical variables, the discriminant groups D1 and D2 are the furthest from all the clay samples. As shown in figure 6.5c the most similar clays (FG4, FG46 and AB334) have D^2 values greater than 44 from the group D1 centroid. The Mahalanobis distances of the clays from the discriminant group D2 (not shown in figure 6.5) are even greater ($D^2 > 68$ for the clay AB334). This is easily explained by the silt-rich nature of the local sediments, opposed to the two mentioned groups, which have clay-rich ceramic bodies.

Greater similarities are found between local clays and the discriminant groups A and C (fig.6.5a and b, respectively). A number of samples fall near the two groups with D^2 values varying between 16 and 40, thus suggesting a certain resemblance between the raw materials and the final products of discriminant groups A and C .

6.5 The raw materials

At this point it is important to mention that the imperfect chemical correspondence between the hypothesised raw materials (clay) and the final products (ceramics) might be due to a local heterogeneity of the clay source. The sampling of 2-3kg of a clay sediment may be not representative of the average composition of the same sediment over a wide area such is a quarry when extensively exploited during tile production. A second reason for the poor correspondence between raw materials and final products could be due to the use of

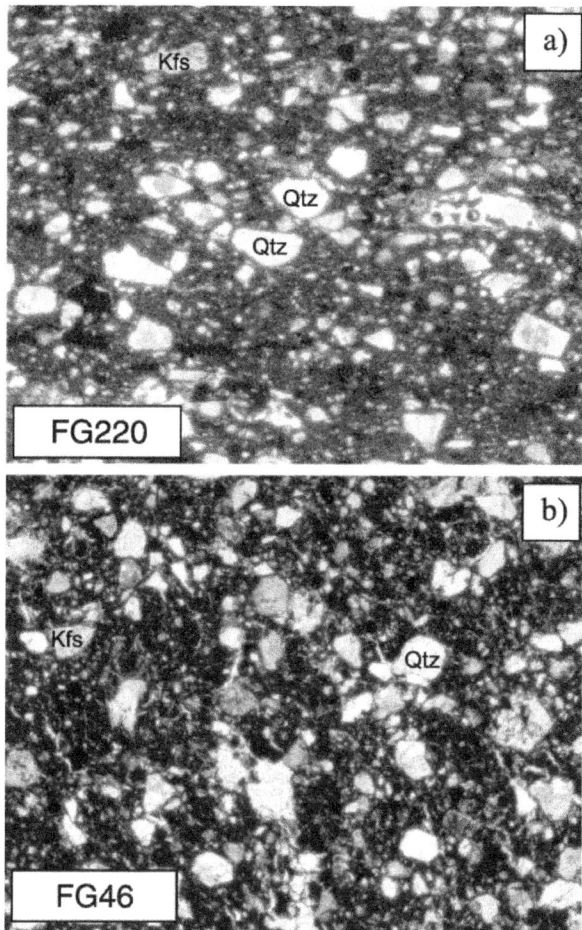

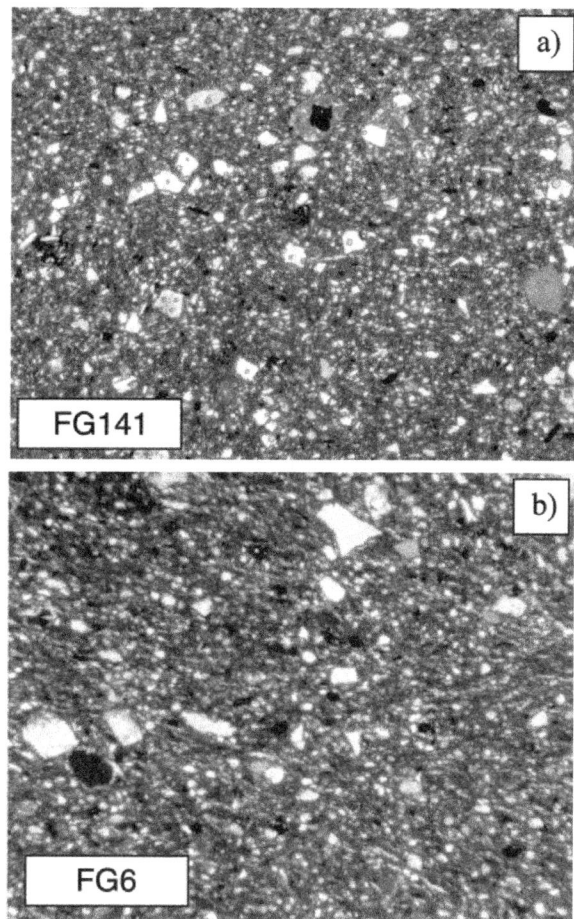

Fig. 6.9: Textural comparison between a representative legionary pot (a) and clay FG46 (b), which is the most similar clay in terms of chemical and petrographic characters. White rectangles are 1mm long.

Fig. 6.10: Textural comparison between the unstamped tile FG141 (a) and clay FG6 (b). This clay is texturally and chemically the most similar one to the two unstamped tiles. White rectangles are 1mm long.

mixed raw materials, as probably done for the tiles of petrographic fabric"b".

In addition, because of the presence of compositional overlap of samples from different areas (paragraph 6.3), the clay provenance cannot be easily determined by means of chemical signature only. This limits the possibilities to correlate the clays and the possible production sites of the tiles from a chemical point of view only. The comparison of petrographic fabrics as well as the archaeological data are required to find out the best correspondences between the final products and their possible raw materials.

6.5.1 Raw materials for the stamped tile production

Comparing the photomicrographs in fig. 6.2 with those in figure 3.1, one can notice that only a small number of clays with a chemical signature similar to the tiles match also from a petrographic point of view. Figures 6.6 and 6.7 show photomicrographs of representative tiles of the discriminant groups A and C and those of some of clays, which fit best regarding chemistry and/or petrography. All photomicrographs are taken at the same

magnification. The tiles of group A display a chemical composition very similar to that of the clays FG46 and FG43. Nevertheless sample FG43 has a fine-grained texture, not observed in the tiles of group A, so that sample FG46 seems the most likely raw material for this group. Other sediments, similar in composition to group A (AB333, AB337, FG43), have larger compositional and textural differences, hence cannot be considered a possible raw material source (see for comparison photomicrographs in fig. 6.2).

The average chemical composition of discriminant group C is most similar to the clay FG4 from Kölliken but also to the clay FG42 and 43 and two clays from the Jura lakes and Avenches (AB334 and AV41: analysis Benghezal, 1994 and Jornet, 1982, respectively). The thin section study, however, allows to exclude clays FG42, FG43, AB334 and AV41 as possible raw materials. As example, figure 6.7b shows that the fine-grained matrix of sample AB334 contains large orthogneiss fragments in a fine-grained clay matrix. This characteristic is always absent in tiles of the discriminant group C. But a good textural resemblance for these tiles is found with the clay FG4 (fig. 6.7c). Both the clay and the tiles show a similar clast/matrix ratio and large dark-brown ARFs with a greywacke texture.

No clays were found that chemically and petrographically match the tiles of discriminant groups D1 and D2.

6.5.2 Raw materials for the other ceramic productions

Because of the small number and heterogeneity of pottery samples and the unstamped tiles of Augustean age, it was impossible to perform statistical analyses to attribute these samples to one of the local clays.

As shown in paragraph 4.4 and figure 4.7, the majority of the pots from Vindonissa are chemically comparable to tiles with petrographic fabric "a" and to those with petrographic fabric "c". Figure 6.8 displays the compositions of the clays, of the two unstamped tiles and of the legionary pots of the 11th legion. The compositional field of the 11th legion's tiles is also reported for comparison. The correspondence among clays and ceramics is not ideal, but the compositions are quite similar for a number of cases. The pots and the two tiles are comparable to various clay samples, in particular to samples FG4, FG6, FG7, FG8 and FG46. However, the petrography does not match for all these samples: therefore it is possible to exclude a relationship with the ceramics for the majority of the considered clays. In fig. 6.9 the photomicrographs of a representative legionary pot is compared to clay FG46 which seems the most similar one if we consider the petrography and the chemistry together. In fig. 6.10 one of the two unstamped tiles (FG141) is compared to the clay FG6 that has rather similar chemical composition and an almost identical petrographic fabric.

As a conclusion, the comparison between the final products and the possible raw materials cannot be based on statistics only, but requires careful consideration of petrographic and chemical aspects, as well as archaeological data (if available). Neglecting one of these steps could be extremely dangerous for the successive interpretation of the results.

In the next chapters, I will formulate some hypotheses about the provenance and technology of Vindonissa ceramics integrating petrographic and chemical data and archaeological information. Actually, the general homogeneity of chemical composition data of the clay does not allow definite conclusions, but the combination of petrographic and archaeological information may exclude or confirm some hypotheses.

Sample ID	Sampling site	Reference	Sample ID	Sampling site	Reference
A89, A91, A92	Augst (BS)	Jornet, 1982	Z128, Z129	Augst (BS)	Maggetti and Galetti, 1994
E75, E76, E77	Bern (BE)	Jornet, 1982	OW42	Oberwinterthur (ZH)	Benghezal, 1989
AV41, AV42	Avenches (FR)	Jornet, 1982	AB334, AB337, AB338, AB342, AB343, AB344, AB352	Region of the Jura lakes	Benghezal, 1994

Table 6.2: List of the Swiss clay samples taken from the literature that were compared with the Vindonissa tiles.

7. Technological aspects of the production

As stated in Nungasser and Maggetti (1978), Maggetti (1986, 1994), Dominuco et al. (1998) and Riccardi et al. (1999), chemical, petrographical and mineralogical analyses provide important information on the processes involved in ceramic production. In the next section I will focus on the technology of the tile production and on the aspect related to the quality of the roman building ceramics.

7.1 Clay processing

For a large group of tiles (petrographic fabric "a", "b", "c"), the analyses pointed out the presence of sandy-silty ceramic bodies. Petrographic compositions obtained by point counting demonstrated that these tiles are "coarse" ceramics with a high volumetric percentage of non-plastic inclusions. These textures are sometimes comparable to those of some fired local clays which were considered possible source materials. For these groups it seems likely that the raw materials were not separated from their coarse component by settling, but were directly used for the ceramic production. This is also demonstrated by the presence of pebbles and large ARFs within the ceramic bodies.

Tiles with petrographic fabric "d" are coarse ceramics like the aforesaid groups, but they display clay-rich textures, never observed in the sampled local sediments. This might suggest that artisans removed the coarse component and then added a controlled percentage of temper to obtain a better ceramic quality. However, the presence of large ARFs, of scattered rounded pebbles (up to 1cm in diameter) and of rounded limestone fragments, contrasts the hypothesis of clay processing. Actually, clay pellets, ARFs and pebbles should not be present in a purified clay. Moreover, the presence of well-rounded limestone fragments within the non-plastic inclusions suggests that these are of sedimentary origin. The roundness of the limestone fragments could be attributed to their lower resistance during the sedimentary transport compared to quartz and feldspar grains. A temper that was added by the craftsmen should have the same roundness factor for all grains (artificial crushing).

7.2 Firing temperature estimation

"...a thermic characterization of this type of firing is impossible due to the considerable variations in temperature in the same firing and even on the same pot...". So wrote Gosselain (1992) about an attempt of characterising the firing conditions during different ethno-archaeological pot firing experiments. Tite (1995) confirms that large variations in the firing temperatures (up to several hundred degrees) might be observed in kiln

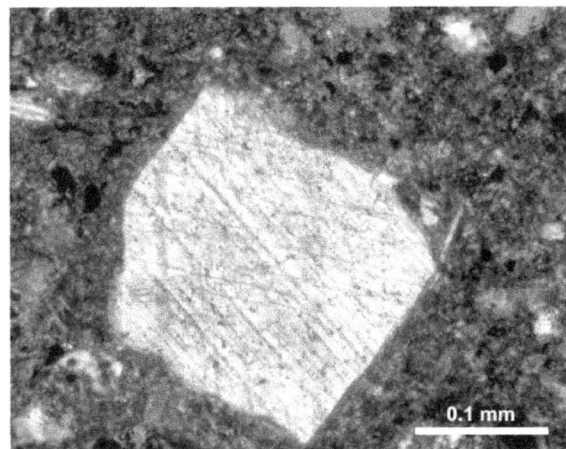

Fig. 7.1: Sample FG95, fabric "b". Primary calcite grain with preserved optical properties. The presence of such grains within the ceramic body implies low firing temperatures and/or short firing times.

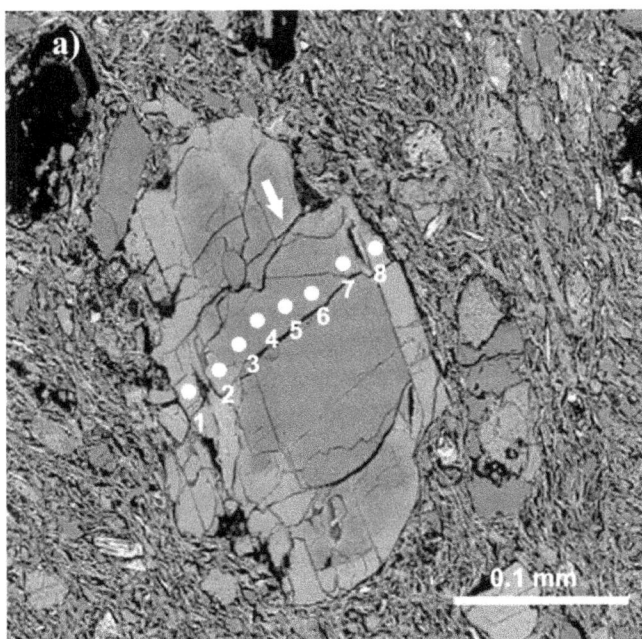

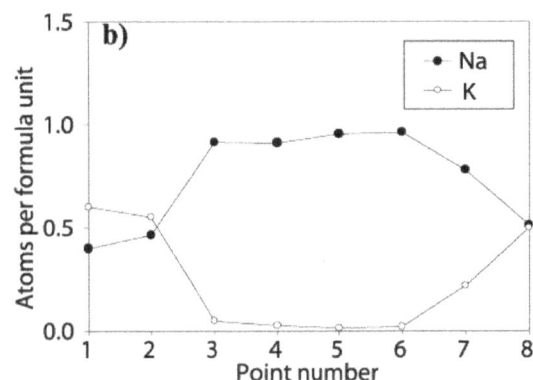

Fig. 7.2: a) Back scattered electron image of a zoned albite grain (sample FG34). Note that the zoning penetrates inside the grains along fractures (white arrow at the upper right of the grain). The white dots indicate microprobe analysis points. As shown in b), the original albite composition (core) undergoes a sharp decrease in Na and an increase in K towards the rim.

41

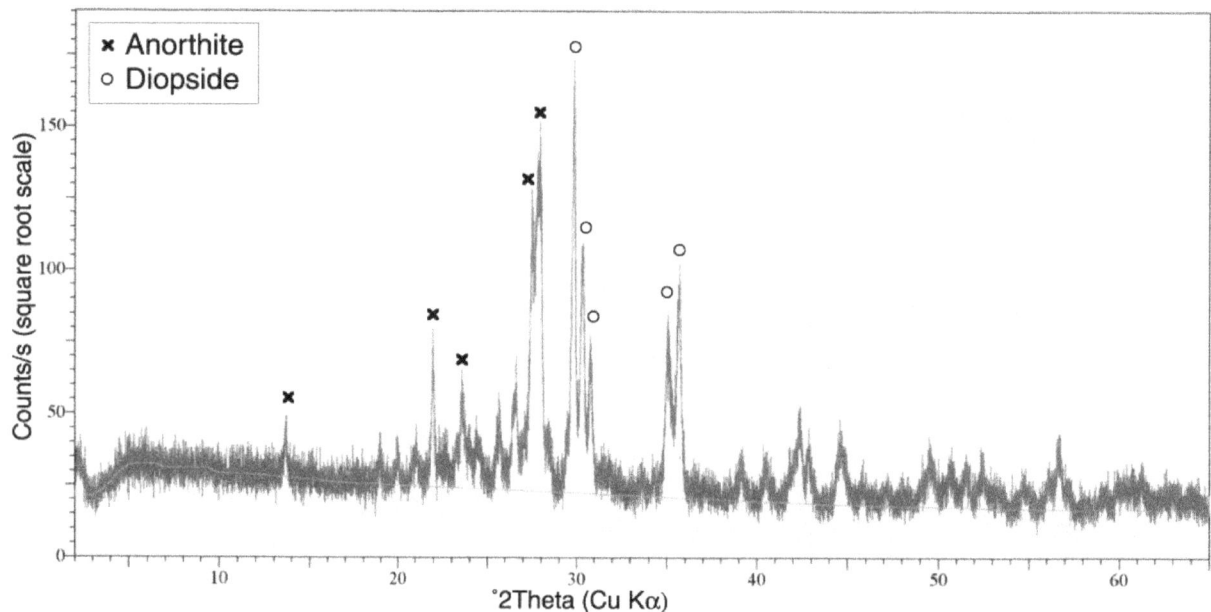

Fig.7.3: XRD analysis at a Ca-rich microdomain (limestone fragment) within sample FG82, stamp type 4 (L·XXIC·). The characteristic peaks of anorthite and diopside are very well developed, indicating firing temperatures > 1050°C (Riccardi et al., 1999).

firings during the same firing within the same vessel. The petrographic and mineralogical observations on the Vindonissa tiles agree with the observations of Gosselain and Tite, since tiles of the same petrographic fabric or chemical group display very different firing textures and mineralogical assemblages. These differences could in some cases account for firing temperature variations of up to 500°C.

Due to these variations, accurate temperature estimation for the Vindonissa tiles is not possible. Anyway it is possible to observe common trends, within groups of tiles

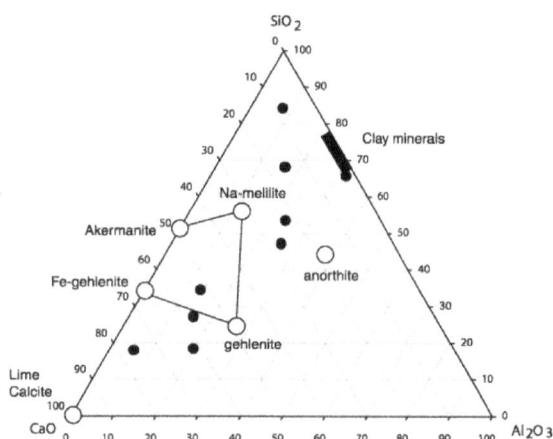

Fig. 7.4: CAS phase diagram (modified from Riccardi et al., 1999) showing the compositions (black dots) after microprobe analyses of non-stoichiometric phases into Ca-rich microdomains (limestone fragments): sample FG19, stamp type 4 (L·XXIC·). The compositions clearly indicate a chemical exchange between two end-members (lime or calcite and clay minerals) producing Ca-silicate phases with compositions approaching those of melilite and anorthite.

or stamps. Some groups display mineralogical features, indicating for medium- to high-temperatures of firing, whereas others have characteristics that can be related to medium or low firing temperatures.

- **Tiles of fabric "a" and "b"**: as already observed, the clay component of these tiles is usually well recognisable under the microscope. Clay minerals as well as the accessory large white-mica flakes commonly preserve their interference colours when viewed under polarised light (fig. 3.1c). Following the literature, optical properties of micas and clay minerals are generally preserved up to 550°C (Riccardi et al., 1999). Moreover, the presence of spathic primary calcite crystals in some samples with petrographic fabric "b" (fig. 7.1) indicates low firing temperatures and/or short firing times. Actually at temperatures exceeding 550°C temperature, calcite starts to decompose into fine-grained aggregates (Riccardi et al. 1999). The presence of spathic calcite suggests that the firing temperatures for these tiles did not exceed 550°C in average or that the firing duration was too short to permit the spathic calcite to decompose into fine-grained calcite.

- **Tiles with petrographic fabric "c" and "d"**: compared to the previous ones, these tiles display other firing textures. The clay minerals in the ceramic bodies are usually not preserved (fig. 3.4d) and the matrix appears to be more uniformly sintered as in the previous groups. X-ray diffraction bulk analyses demonstrate that the hematite peak are present whereas the illite peaks may lack. Chlorite peaks are always absent. Albite crystals are mostly zoned at their rim and along fractures. Electron microprobe analyses reveal that the zoning consists of domains enriched in the K-feldspar component (fig.7.2). As demonstrated by Dominuco et al. (1998), such zoned rims are the result of a mutual exchange of K and Na between albite and clay minerals. The zoning penetrates into the grain probably driven by a fluid phase released during clay dehydratation.

XRD analyses on limestone fragments, representing Ca-rich microdomains (Maggetti, 1986), show that in some samples the assemblage quartz + calcite is stable. In these cases, calcite is always transformed into fine-grained aggregates. In other samples, commonly represented by the tiles with stamp type 4, the micro domains consist of the assemblage diopside + anorthite (fig. 7.3) or diopside + calcite. Anorthite and diopside are attested to develop at about 1050°C from a reaction involving SiO_2, CaO and the clay minerals (Riccardi et al., 1999). Electron microprobe analyses at such microdomains often gave non-stoichiometric compositions falling between calcite and anorthite, into the melilite field, as shown in fig. 7.4. Actually, within the sample of this group (fabric "c" and d"), the tiles with stamp type 4 (L·XXIC·) appear to be the most highly sintered.

Based on the previous observations, a rough estimation of the firing temperatures for tiles with petrographic fabric "c" and "d" can be proposed:

i)   the usual presence of the hematite peaks constrains the lower temperature to about 600°C (Maggetti, 1982).

ii)   The average firing temperatures of these groups can be constrained around 750°-950°C, as shown by:

- The common presence of fine-grained calcite aggregates, which may be preserved up to 750-850°C (Heimann, 1989, Riccardi et al., 1999).

- The K-feldspar rims around albite grains, starting to develop at temperatures exceeding

850°C (Dominuco et al., 1998).

- The rare presence of the main illite peaks, which commonly begin to disappear at temperature over 900°C (Maggetti, 1982).

iii)   The uncommon presence of diopside + anorthite assemblages indicates that in some cases (generally for the tiles with stamp type 4) temperatures above 1050°C were reached.

7.3 Quantification of the production

7.3.1 Estimation of the produced tiles

The archaeological studies at Vindonissa (Jahn, 1909; Hartmann, 1986; Fellmann, 1988; Meyer-Freuler, 1998) indicate that during the second half of the first century the Vindonissa camp could accomodate about 6000 soldiers. The camp consisted of 15 barracks, thermal baths, a hospital, a warehouse, residences for the officers and administrative buildings (fig. 7.5). I roughly estimated the roof surface of all these building, by considering archaeological data and maps given by Hartmann (1986). Considering only the surface covered by a roof (inside courts were not taken into account), the total roof-covered surface of the 11th legion's camp exceeded 51000 m^2.

The calculation of the roof surface depends on the roof pitch. Based on Shirley (1996), a roof pitch of 20° was used for the calculation. Actually, the Vindonissa tiles were not fixed with nails to the timber structure (Jahn, 1909), so that a larger pitch is unlikely, because it would have posed stability problems. As stated in Shirley (1996), the arrangement of the roof slopes of complex buildings, such as the Tribune's houses, has only little influence on the number of tiles used. To simplify the calculation, I considered that all buildings had a gabled roof (Fig.7.6). In this way, it was possible to assume that the camp was made by simple rectangular buildings. I first considered an ideal barrack, which has dimensions of 15x80m and a roof surface of about 1280 m^2. A *tegula* has an average surface of 0.1575 m^2 (Jahn, 1909; Fetz and Meyer-Freuler, 1997). The roof structure implies that two successive *tegulae* are partially overlap: assuming an overlapping of 5 cm, the surface covered by each *tegula* reduces to only 0.14m^2. According to this scheme, approximately 9100 tegulae and 9600 imbrices were necessary for the roof of an ideal barrack. Considering the presence of overhanging verges, with a 30 cm overhang, the number of used tiles would increase by approximately 4-5%. Assuming that the camp was entirely composed of   ideal barracks, approximately 390000 *tegulae* and 408000 *imbrices* were necessary to cover 51000 m^2 of building surface. Since a *tegula* weighs an average of 11 kg (Jahn, 1909) and an *imbrex* approx. 3.3 kg (Fetz and Meyer-Freuler, 1997),

Fig. 7.5: Reconstruction of the Vindonissa legionary camp at the end of the first century AD (model in the Vindonissa Museum, Brugg). In this period, the camp could accommodate up to 6000 soldiers.

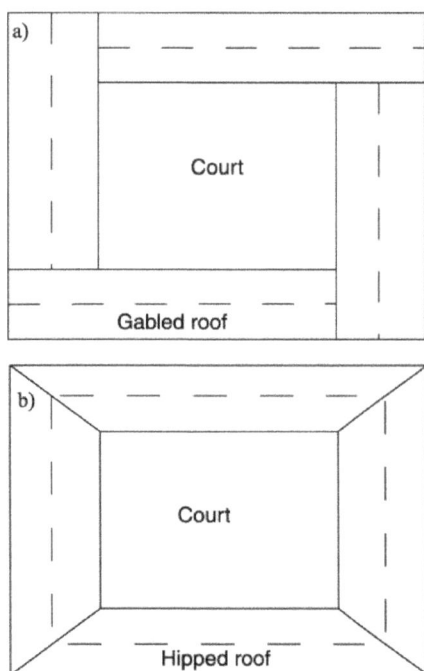

Fig. 7.6: Schematic plans of a Tribune's house, with two different roof slopes arrangement, modified from Shirley (1996). a) Gabled roof; b) Hipped roof. Following Shirley (1996), the two arrangements produce negligible differences in the quantity of roof coverings.

approximatively 5600 tons of tiles should have been produced only for the Vindonissa legionary camp.

7.3.2 Firing and fuel consumption estimation

The Roman tile kilns commonly had a square shape with a length between 2.5 and 3 m and a height between 2 and 3 m (Arnold, 1963; Le Ny 1988 and 1998). Le Ny (1988) calculated that about 260 tiles would fit in a 2 m³ volume. This implies that 1600-2400 tiles could be fired at once in an ordinary kiln. In addition the author assumes that a firing in Roman times lasted at least two weeks, with one week entirely devoted to increasing the furnace

temperature and one week to let the kiln cool down.

A firing experiment using a replicate medieval kiln (Wolf, 1999) showed that 8 days of firing and about 12.5 tons of wood were necessary to reach a maximal firing temperature of 800-1000°C in the kiln. As the dimension of this replicate medieval kiln (3x3x3m) is comparable to that of a Roman tile kiln, we can assume that the duration of the firing and the quantity of fuel used apply also to Roman kilns. Considering an average number of 2000 tiles per firing, nearly 200 firing events lasting two weeks each, were necessary for the production of Vindonissa *tegulae* only. Taking into account the potential imprecision of this estimation, I calculated the use of approximatively 2400 tons of fuel to complete all the firings.

7.4 Quality of the Roman tiles

To compare the technical properties of the archaeological tiles with those of the actual products standard quality tests were performed on a restricted number of tile specimens. Due to the destructive character of these tests and the large quantity of material needed, it was only possible to carry out the analyses on a few specimens. The tests on resistance to flexion, i.e. bending strength and to freeze-thaw cycling, were performed with the technical support of the tile factory Zürcher Ziegeleien Wancor (see annexe B6). In addition, porosimetric analyses were carried out at the Institute of Mineralogy of Fribourg. As shown in table 7.1, the resistance to flexion of the seven samples analysed is very different.

Five samples broke after the loading value requested for the actual production (1000 N). The other samples display lower values. The bending strength is, in contrast, always lower when compared to that of the actual production (about 12 N/mm², for a tile 12-15mm thick).

Sample ID	Stamp type	Width (mm)	Thickness (mm)	Breaking load (N)	Bending strength (N/mm²)
FG15	3	41.09	32.85	1752	5.93
FG18	4	35.43	27.52	1746	9.76
FG51	1	33.63	31.15	1589	7.30
FG56	2	31.40	25.35	557	4.14
FG70	2	30.12	34.15	343	1.46
FG123	14	30.70	28.12	1139	7.04
FG120	2	33.21	29.40	1077	5.63
FG71	13	-	-	n.a.	n.a.
FG73	13	-	-	n.a.	n.a.

Table 7.1: Resistance to flexion of the archaeological samples. The standard values requested for the modern products are 1000N breaking load and 12N/mm² bending strenght. Five samples display breaking load and bending strenght values respectively higher and lower than the standard ones.
n.a.: not analysed.

This is explained by the fact that the resistance to flexion is directly proportional to the breaking load and inversely proportional to the squared thickness of the specimen. The thickness of the Vindonissa tiles is two to three times that of a modern tile, which generally displays comparable breaking loads.

Table 7.2 displays the results of the freezing resistance test on the previous seven samples and on two additional tiles with stamp type 13. In this case also, the results were worse than the standard values required for modern ceramic tiles. The two tiles with stamp type 13 gave the best results since they survived five of the ten control steps of the standard test without damages. The porosimetric analyses, carried out on 104 samples, showed that the tiles have an average open porosity of 33% (see annexe F for the results). This open microporosity values are similar to the modern products (micro-porosity in average = 30%). The weak behaviour of the roman tiles is then most likely due to the presence of large macropores (up to some millimetres) also visible on the macroscopic sample. Actually, the slower freezing resistance can be explained by water percolating inside the macropores of the ceramics. Under wet and cold climatic conditions, with alternance of freezing and thaw cycles, this high porosity produces a quick ageing of the ceramic product.

With respect to the physical properties, the Roman tiles seem to be a medium to low quality product. The craftsmen were probably aware of the weakness of their products and were forced to produce very thick tiles (on average 3cm, sometimes up to 4cm) to compensate for the low strength. However, the low resistance to mechanical loading could partly be attributed to the long burial which commonly produces an alteration of the ceramic body and a weakening of the sintered matrix (Heimann and Maggetti, 1981).

Table 7.2: Resistance to freezing conditions of the archaeological samples. All samples showed important damages or even broke before the end of the standard test (150 cycles). The sample shape as well as locations and shapes of damages are schematically represented.

45

8. Data discussion

In this chapter, an interpretation of the data presented in the previous chapters is provided. Petrographic, chemical and statistical analyses demonstrated that the Vindonissa tiles divide into several groups, possibly related to different production sites. It is important to mention that it was not possible to formulate a hypothesis about the origin of each of the groups of tiles. Moreover, since the distinction among the groups and their attribution to a local source was in most cases only possible through a multi-analytical approach, I avoided to define reference groups based on the chemical composition only.

8.1 Provenance of ceramics

8.1.1 Tiles of group A and unclassified tiles with petrographic fabric "b"

The tiles classified into the group A are comparable to a rather common clay (FG46) from Rupperswil, both in terms of petrographic fabric and chemical compositions. These tiles, showing the stamp type 12 (L·XXI·L) and in rare case the stamp type 13, are rather rare among the archaeological finds of Vindonissa and have a very limited distribution in the legionary camp and in the *villa rustica* of Seeb (ZH). These two indications allow interpreting these tiles as a regional production of minor importance. The production site of the tiles of group A should be localised in the area between Rupperswil and Vindonissa, and the raw material used was presumably a clay very similar to the clay sample FG46. Unfortunately, there is no archaeological evidence to support this hypothesis, since no tiles of these types were found near any of the known Roman kilns. A similar hypothesis may be formulated for the unclassified tiles with stamp type 13 (section 5.2). These tiles are composed of a heterogeneous clay, consisting of a mixing of a calcareous clay and a clay similar to that used for the tiles of group A.

8.1.2 Tiles of group D1

The archaeological kiln complex of Rupperswil has been always considered an important production site for Vindonissa tiles (Arnold, 1969; Fellmann, 1988), because a number of stamped wasters of the two legions have been found near the kiln complex. At least for the tiles of group D1, based on the presented data, two arguments appear to confirm this hypothesis. First, the only analysed waster coming from Rupperswil (FG140, 11th legion) was classified in the petrographic fabric "d" as the majority of tiles bearing "Rupperswil stamps". In addition, as shown by discriminant analysis, the waster falls near the centroid of discriminant group D1; i.e. its chemical composition is similar to the average chemical composition of this

group. The second argument is the extreme homogeneity of the "Rupperswil tiles". Even if sampled at different archaeological sites of Switzerland, 94% of tiles bearing one of the stamps found at Rupperswil display similar petrographic and chemical characteristics. An analogous behaviour is easily explained by a common origin for all these ceramics: an identical source of raw materials and a similar technology is obviously at the base of this production. It is possible to attribute to the same raw material source the majority of the tiles of the 21st legion and all those of the 11th legion. Also, the 6th cohort *Raetorum* most likely produced its tiles here. Concerning the tiles of the 21st legion, it is assumed that all tiles with stamp types 1,2,3 and 9 except three unclassified cases (FG10, FG150, FG198), and three samples which clearly belong to group C (FG11, FG22, FG99) were produced at Rupperswil. In addition, 17 tiles with the stamp type 4 (L·XXIC·) are probably to attribute to this group (section 5.2), even if no archaeological evidence may confirm this hypothesis. Finally, also one frontal tile (FG143) belong to the Rupperswil production. Table 8.1 reports all samples attributed to group D, which are assumed to be produced in Rupperswil. None of the local clays analysed can be considered a possible raw material source for the production at Rupperswil. All tiles of this group are characterised by lower non-plastic inclusion contents in the ceramic body than that of the sampled clays. If we accept that the clay used in the tile production was not processed, two arguments may explain the impossibility to find out the raw material used at this production site:

i)   the local clay sampling was not successful because the raw material is an uncommon source in the region;

ii)   the raw material has been totally consumed by the Roman or later productions.

8.1.3 Tiles of group D2

This group of tiles, all with the stamp L·XXIC· (type 4), has a very peculiar chemical composition, showing very high Ni and Cr contents. Neither the Swiss ceramic reference groups nor the local clays display compositions similar to the group D2. In addition, there is no archaeological evidence yet for a production centre for these tiles. Actually, wasters with these stamps were never found near the known kilns. With respect to their chemical composition it is possible to exclude a provenance from Rupperswil and Kölliken, but I cannot suggest another possible production site. Fuchs and Margueron (1998) state that a production centre for all tiles stamped L·XXIC· could be located in the region of the Jura lakes. This could explain the spread of these tiles throughout Western Switzerland (Fuchs and Margueron, 1998), but I have no proof to confirm this hypothesis. My results show that the tiles with the stamp L·XXIC· split into two different chemical groups. The first grouping (17 tiles) most likely belongs to the Rupperswil production whereas the group D2 formed by 13 tiles with unusual chemical composition, remains without a possible production centre.

Object	Sample ID
21st legion tiles	FG12, FG13, FG14, FG15, FG20, FG21, FG41, FG47, FG49, FG51, FG52, FG55, FG56, FG62, FG63, FG64, FG65, FG66, FG70, FG73, FG76, FG82, FG83, FG84, FG85, FG86, FG87, FG89, FG97, FG100, FG101, FG103, FG105, FG106, FG107, FG108, FG109, FG116, FG117, FG119, FG120, FG144, FG147, FG148, FG155, FG156, FG157, FG160, FG161, FG162, FG165, FG166, FG167, FG168, FG172, FG173, FG184, FG185, FG186, FG187, FG188, FG189, FG191, FG193, FG197, FG199
11th legion tiles	FG26, FG27, FG28, FG29, FG30, FG31, FG32, FG53, FG54, FG58, FG67, FG68, FG69, FG78, FG79, FG80, FG81, FG88, FG92, FG93, FG94, FG102, FG104, FG111, FG112, FG113, FG114, FG118, FG121, FG122, FG123, FG140, FG163, FG164, FG169, FG170, FG171, FG183, FG194, FG195
6th cohort tiles	FG34, FG38, FG50, FG72
Frontal tile	FG143

Table 8.1: List of the samples that were produced at Rupperswil, considered the main production site for Vindonissa tiles.

8.1.4 Tiles of group C

As shown by the petrographic and discriminant analyses, the tiles attributed to group C have similar characteristics to the clay FG4 which was sampled at Kölliken about 25 km SW from Vindonissa. In the historical introduction (section 1.5), I pointed out that a tile kiln was found at Kölliken, thus there is evidence of tile production at Kölliken. However there is no agreement among archaeologists about the period of activity of this workshop. We should remember that nearly all the tiles produced by the auxiliary cohorts (except those of the cohort 6th *Raetorum*, stamp type 5) and three tiles of the 21st legion *rapax* belong to the discriminant group C. The resemblance of these tiles with the clay FG4 from Kölliken seems to agree with the interpretation of Hartmann and Speidel (1991). These authors infer that the tile kiln were probably used by the 21st legion and by the auxiliary cohorts. With this in mind, it is likely that the 3rd, 7th and 26th cohorts produced their tiles at Kölliken. Also the 21st legion probably produced a small part of its tiles there. In addition, the presence of four *antefixa* surely belonging to the group C plus other three

which probably belong to it (section 5.2), suggest that the kiln of Kölliken was also in charge to produce a part of these ornamental tiles. If we consider that the auxiliary cohorts were present at Vindonissa at different times, we can also assume that the kilns of Kölliken and Rupperswil were not in use at the same time. Considering also the archaeological data (section 1.5), it is possible to hypothesise that the centre of Kölliken began to produce already for the 7th and 26th cohorts and continued to work until the arrival of the 3rd cohort *Hispanorum*.

8.1.5 The legionary pots of the 11th legion

There is no archaeological evidence of a production site for the legionary pots at Vindonissa (Ettlinger and Simonnet, 1952; Ettlinger, 1998). These pots are some of the most common finds of Flavian age, and archaeologists agree that they represent the remnants of an important production. Moreover, the occurrence of these ceramics is mostly concentrated in the Vindonissa legionary camp: only a few examples are known from other archaeological sites (generally military posts) around the camp, for example in Baden-*Aquae Helveticae*. As discussed in the previous chapter, the composition of "legionary pots" from Vindonissa are generally similar to some local clays, and to the tiles of group A and C. It is thus possible to extend the assumption made for these tiles also to the pottery of the 11th legion. Like the tiles of group A and C, the pots may be considered a local productions that came from the region between Kölliken and Vindonissa and were made with raw materials, easily accessible in the region.

8.1.6 Unstamped tiles

As introduced in Chapter 2, the two unstamped tiles come from the archaeological excavation of the legionary camp, but they belong to an older phase (Augustean times), for which no tile production is attested. I demonstrated that the chemical compositions of the two samples are comparable to those of a number of local clays sampled in the region around the camp. Moreover, the petrographic fabric is almost identical to that of the clay FG6, sampled at Lupfig (AG), about four kilometres SW of the legionary camp. With this in mind, but without ignoring that the number of analysed samples is far from a statistical significance, it can be assumed that the two samples are of local origin. This could demonstrate that tile production was already established in pre-military times although not extensively diffused.

8.1.7 The unattributed samples

As shown in table 5.2 after discriminant analysis, only few cases remained without an attribution after discriminant analysis. By excluding the samples with petrographic fabric "b", for which an hypothesis has already been formulated in paragraph 8.1.1, the impossibility to classify the other samples may be often related to contamination problems. Actually three of the five unattributed samples have high phosporous contents and were considered contaminated (FG135, FG150, FG217). With regard to the last two unattributed samples (FG10 and FG126), the petrographic analysis suggests a possible (but not sure) similarity to the petrographic fabric "d". The type of stamp suggests for the sample FG10 a possible origin from Rupperswil. The sample FG126 is a frontal tile. No archaeological hypothesis can be formulated about its provenance. I suggest that for these two cases the observed peculiar characteristics should rather be attributed to a casual sample heterogeneity than to an unknown production site.

8.2 Technology of the tile production

It is interesting to linger over the implications of the tile production in the region. As stated in Hartmann (1986), during the last half of the first century AD, the legionary camp should have been an immense building yard. The tile production largely exceeding 5000 tons would have required accurate logistics and a huge manpower potential to provide raw materials and fuel as well as to fabricate and then transport the ceramics from the workshops to the camp. Most likely, the production was much more intense than calculated. In chapter 7, the rough estimation takes into account only the tiles produced to cover the legionary camp, as we know it today. The Vindonissa tiles were, however, distributed to a number of other Swiss archaeological sites, mainly little military posts and villas, such as in Alpnach and Seeb.

As shown by the differences found in the chemo-petrographic characteristics of the tiles, the proportion of this archaeo-industrial production most likely required different kilns active to support the request. This is evident during the first years of occupation of the camp, when the 21st legion and the cohorts probably had 3-4 different sites of production. When the 11th legion replaced the 21st legion, the camp was already partially built and the tile production was most likely limited to repair the ancient building and to build new ones. In this last period the production centre at Rupperswil was then probably sufficient to support the demand.

9. Conclusions

With respect to the questions posed in Chapter 1 and taking into account the discussion of the data in Chapter 8, we can briefly summarise the results of this work as follows:

I) The Vindonissa stamped tiles do not form a homogeneous group. I could establish chemically and petrographically distinct groups. These groups do not relate to the archaeological site of finding, but mainly to the stamp type: tiles with the same stamp type display similar petrographic and chemical characteristics even if they were found at different archaeological sites. This suggests that the export of the tiles from one production centre to different sites was a common practice. The production of the 21st legion and its auxiliary cohorts can be subdivided into four petrographic and chemical groups, which often relate to stamp types or groups of stamp type. This suggests that the differences in stamp type could be related to different production periods and/or different production sites. The production of the 11th legion is rather homogeneous and the different stamp types display the same textural and chemical characteristics.

II) Several production sites may be suggested for the Vindonissa tiles. The majority of these stamped tiles have been produced and fired at two workshops located at Rupperswil and Kölliken. Rupperswil was the main production centre for the 21st legion *rapax* and the 11th legion *claudia pia fidelis*, as well as for the 6th cohort *Raetorum*. The kiln in Kölliken was the main production centre for the 7th cohort *Raetorum*, the 26th cohort *volontariorum civium Romanorum* and for the 3rd cohort *Hispanorum*. The 21st legion probably also used the kiln at Kölliken for a short time. A production site in the region between Rupperswil and Vindonissa is also proposed for the tiles of the 21st legion with stamp type 12 and 13, and for the legionary pots of the 11th legion. The site could not be localised, but the characteristics of the ceramics, as well as their occurrence in few sites around the camp suggest their local origin. Finally, some tiles with the stamp type 4 (21st legion) have a peculiar chemical signature that cannot be attributed to any of the suggested production sites. It was not possible to determine the origin of these tiles.

III) The tiles of the 21st and 11th legion from the Swiss sites are remarkably different from the tiles of the same legions found in Strasbourg and Rottweil, respectively. This suggests that the export of tiles from Vindonissa did not reach the sites north of the Rhine waterfalls, and that the production was limited to the period the military units stayed at Vindonissa. The compositions of the Vindonissa tiles are also easily distinguishable from the military tiles from *Augusta Raurica* produced by the 1st legion

Martiorum. This indicates that each military camp had its own production site(s) and commonly used local raw material sources (see also Maggetti and Galetti, 1994).

IV) The craftsmen usually did not process the clays to produce the tiles and the legionary pots. The Roman roof coverings are ceramics of medium to low quality. As the craftsmen were probably conscious of the limited quality, they produced very thick tiles to compensate for the intrinsic weakness of the products. In contrast to this, the legions demonstrated a considerable logistic organisation to produce and then distribute huge quantities of ceramics up to several dozens of kilometres from the production sites.

Acknowledgements

This work is part of my PhD research. I would like to thank my supervisor prof. Marino Maggetti, who suggested the study topic and gave me the possibility to carry out the research work at the Institute of Mineralogy and Petrography, University of Fribourg. Prof. Robert Heimann and Dr. Mike Baxter are kindly acknowledged for the careful reviews on both concept and content of the original manuscript.
I am especially grateful to :
- prof. Bernard Grobety, Dr. Vincent Serneels the helpful discussions;
- prof. Giulio Galetti for the technical support during sample preparation, and for performing chemical analyses;
- Mrs. Odette Marbacher for the help during laboratory-work;
- Mr. Jean Paul Bourqui de Fribourg for the preparation of thin-sections.
Thanks are also due to the archaeologists of the Archaeological Cantonal Service of Aargau, in particular to Mrs. Christine Mayer-Freuler and Mr. René Hänngi who provided the majority of the samples and who were always at disposal for questions and discussion.
The Zürcher Ziegeleien Zwankor and Dr. Thomas Mumenthaler are kindly acknowledged for the support during technical tests on tiles.
I acknowledge support for the electron microprobe of the University of Bern by Schweizer Nationalfonds (Credit 21-26579.89)

References

Adams, A. E., Mackenzie, W.S., Guilford, C., 1988. *Atlas of Sedimentary Rocks under the Microscope*. Longman Group Ltd.

Arnold, P., 1966. Die Römische Ziegeleien von Hunzenschwil-Rupperswil. *Jahresberichte Gesellschaft pro-Vindonissa 1965*, 37-53.

Baxter, M. J., 1992. Statistical analysis of chemical compositional data and the comparison of analyses. *Archaeometry*, 2(34), 267-277.

Baxter, M. J., 1994. *Exploratory multivariate analysis in archaeology*. Edinburg University Press, Edinburg.

Baxter, M. J., 1994. Stepwise discriminant analysis in archaeometry: a Critique. *Journal of Archaeological Sciences* (21), 659-666.

Baxter, M. J., 1999. Detecting multivariate outliers in artefact compositional data. *Archaeometry*, 2(41), 321-338.

Baxter, M. J., 2001. Statistical modelling of artefact compositional data. *Archaeometry*, 1(43), 131-147.

Bearat, H., Dufournier D., 1994. Quelques experiences sur la fixation du Phosphore par les ceramiques. *Revue d'Archéometrie*, 18, 65-73.

Benghezal, A., 1989. Groupes de reference des poiteries gallo-romaines de Seeb (ZH-Suisse) et Oberwinterthur (ZH-Suisse): Caractéristiques mineralogiques, chimiques et techniques. *Unpublished Diploma-work, University of Fribourg, Switzerland.*

Benghezal, A., 1990. Les poteries gallo-romaines de Seeb: analyses chimiques et mineralogiques. *In: W. Drack et al., Die römische Gutshof bei Seeb. Ausgrabungen 1958-1969. Berichte der Zürcher Denkmalpflege*, 8 (Arch. Monogr.), 240-253.

Bohn, O., 1925. Hölzerne Schrifttafeln aus Vindonissa. *Germania* 9, 43-45

Brodribb, G., Cleere, H., 1988. The classis Britannica bath-house at Beauport Park, East Sussex. *Britannia*(19), 217-274.

Cogswell, J. W., Neff, H. , Glascock, D., 1996. The effect of firing temperature on the elemental characterization of pottery. *Journal of Archaeological Science*, 23, 283-387.

Collomb, P., Maggetti, M., 1996. Dissolution des phosphates présents dans des céramiques contaminées. *Revue d'Archéometrie*(20), 69-75.

Courtois, L., Velde, B., 1984. Application de l'analyse quantitative à la microsonde electronique, à l'étude des céramiques archéologiques. *PACT*, 10, 365-371.

Cuomo di Caprio, N., Vaughan S.J., 1993. An experimental study in distinguishing grog (chamotte) from argillaceous inclusions in ceramic thin sections. *Archaeometry*, 7(1), 21-40.

Dolata, J., 1996. Hin zu einer archäologischen Nutzanwendung geochemischer Analytik römischer Baukeramik. *Mainzer Archäologische Zeitschrift*(3), 105-125.

Dolata, J., 2000. Römische Ziegelstempel aus Mainz und dem nördlichen Obergermanien - Archäologische und archäometrische Untersuchungen zu chronologischem und baugeschichtlichem Quellenmaterial. *Unpublished PhD Thesis, J.W. Goethe Universität, Frankfurt am Main.*

Dominuco, P., Messiga, B., Riccardi, M.P., 1998. Firing process of natural clays. Some microtexture and related phase compositions. *Thermochimica Acta*, 321, 185-190.

Dondi, M., Ercolani, G., Fabbri, B., Marsigli, M., 1998. An approach to the chemistry of pyroxenes formed during firing of Ca-rich silicate ceramics. *Clay Minerals*, 33, 443-452.

Drack, W., 1975. *Ur- und Frühgeschichtliche Archaeologie der Schweiz - Die römische Epoche*. Verlag Schweiz. Gesellschaft für Ur- und Frühgeschichte, Basel.

Drack, W., Fellmann, R., Meyer-Freuler, C., Benghezal, A., Dettwiler-Brown, D., Hedinger, B., Brem, H., Leibundgut, A., Roth-Rubi, K., Rütti, B., 1987. Der römische Gutshof bei Seeb, Gemeinde Winkel. *Monographien der Kantonsarchäologie*, 8.

Duruz, M., Maggetti, M. (1997): An Early Medieval pottery workshop from the 9th Century at Reinach/Switzerland. *Proceedings of the 31th Archaeometry Symposium 1997, Budapest*, in press.

Ettlinger, E., 1951. Legionary pottery from Vindonissa. *Journal of Roman Studies* 41, 105-111.

Ettlinger, E., Simonnet, C., 1952. Römische Keramik aus dem Schütthugel von Vindonissa. *Veröffentlichungen der Gesellschaft pro-Vindonissa*, 3.

Ettlinger, E., 1998. Noch einmal zur Keramik der 11. Legion in Vindonissa. *Jahresberichte Gesellschaft pro-Vindonissa (1997)*, 37-46.

Fellmann, R., 1988. *La Suisse gallo-romaine - Cinq siècles d'histoire*. Payot, Lausanne.

Fetz, H., Meyer-Freuler, C., 1997. Triengen, Murhübel. *Archäologische Schriften Luzern*(7), 370-442.

Fetz, H., 1998. Römischer Ziegelbrennofen in Triengen. *Ziegelei Museum*, **13**, 17-24.

Fischer, P., 1987. Formation of the ceramic body in heavy clay products during firing. *Ziegeleitechnisches Jahrbuch*, 96-108.

Franke, R., 1998. Ein Lager der legion XI Claudia in Arae Flaviae/Rottweil und die Besetzung des oberen Neckartales. *Jahresberichte Gesellschaft pro-Vindonissa (1997)*, 25-32.

Fuchs, M., Margueron, G., 1998. Les estampilles sur tuiles d'Avenches. Afranius, la légion XXI, Cornelius, Camillius et les autres. *Bullettin de l'Association Pro-Aventico*(4), 105-172.

von Gonzenbach, V., 1963. Die Verbreitung der gestempelten Ziegel der im 1. Jahrhundert in Vindonissa liegenden römischen Truppen. *Bonner Jahresberichte*, **163**, 79-150.

Gosselain, O. P., 1992. Bonfire of the enquiries: pottery firing temperature in Archaeology: what for? *Journal of Archaeological Science*, **19**, 243-259.

Hardmeyer, B., Osterwalder Maier, C., Morschi, A., 1993. Eine lange Geschichte - kurz gefasst: 1500km Autobahn und 50000 Jahre Geschichte. *Interner Zwischenbericht der Archäologischen Zentralstelle für den Nationalstrassenbau*.

Hartmann, M., 1986. *Vindonissa - Oppidum, Legionslager, Castrum*. Gemeinderat Windisch, Brugg, AG.

Hartmann, M., Speidel M.A., 1991. Die Hilfscohorten des Windischer Heeresverbandes. *Jahresberichte Gesellschaft pro-Vindonissa*.

Heighway, C. M., Parker, A.J., 1982. The Roman tilery at St Oswald's Priory, Gloucester. *Britannia*(13), 25-77.

Heimann, R. B., Maggetti, M., 1981. Experiments on simulated burial of calcareous terra sigillata (mineralogical change). Preliminary results. *British Museum occasional paper*, **19**, 163-177.

Heimann, R. B., 1989. Assessing the technology of ancient pottery: the use of ceramic phase diagrams. *Archaeomaterials*, **3**(2), 123-148.

Hertli, U., Maggetti, M., Jornet, A., Galetti, G., 1999. Where was the Terra Sigillata workshop of *FLORUS*? *Proceedings of the 4th European Meeting on Ancient Ceramics, Archaeological and Archaeometrical Studies, Andorra 1997*, 168-174.

Howald, E., Meyer, E., 1940. *Die Römische Schweiz*, Zürich.

Irvine, T.N., Rumble III, D., 1992. A writing guide for petrological (and other geological) manuscripts. *Journal of Petrology*, **22**, 1-46.

Isler, A., Pasquier, F., Huber, M., 1984. Geologische Karte der zentralen Nordschweiz - 1:100000, NAGRA-Scweizerischen geologischen Kommission.

Jahn, V., 1909. Die römischen Dachziegel aus Windisch. *Anzeiger für Altertumskunde*, 111-129.

Jolliffe, I. T., 1986. *Principal Component Analysis*. Springer-Verlag.

Jornet, A., 1980. Composition de la céramique romaine d'Augusta Raurica (Augst). *Schweiz.Min.Petr.Mitt.*, **60**, 271-285.

Jornet, A., 1982. Analyse minéralogique et chimique de la céramique romaine en Suisse à enduit brillant. *Unpublished PhD Thesis, University of Fribourg, Switzerland*, **n°846**.

Kilikoglu, V., Maniatis, Y. and Grimanis, A.P., 1988. The effect of purification and firing of clays on trace element provenance studies. *Archaeometry*, **30**(1), 37-46.

Klecka, W. R., 1987. *Discriminant Analysis*. SAGE Publications.

Le Bohec, Y., 1989. L'armée romaine. *Gnomon*, **64**, 328-337.

Le Ny, F., 1988. *Les fours de tuiliers gallo-romains - Methodologie, étude technologique, typologique et statistique, chronologie*. Maison des Sciences de l'Homme, Paris.

Le Ny, F., 1998. Le fours de tuilieres gallo-romains en Suisse. *Ziegelei Museum*, **15**, 23-30.

Lemoine, C., Picon, M., 1981. La fixation du phosphore par les céramiques lors de leur enfuissement et ses incidentes analytiques. *Revue d'Archéometrie*, **6**, 110-112.

Letsch, E. e. a., 1907. Die schweizerischen Tonlager. *Beitrage zur Geologie der Schweiz, Geotechnische Serie*, **IV**.

Maggetti, M., 1981. Composition of Roman pottery from Lousonna (Switzerland). *British Museum Occasional Paper*, **19**, 33-49.

Maggetti, M., 1982. Phase analysis and its significance for technology and origin. *Archaeological Ceramics*, 121-133.

Maggetti, M., Schwab, H., 1982. Iron age fine pottery from Châtillon-s-Glâne and the Heuneburg. *Archaeometry*, **24**(1), 21-36.

Maggetti, M., Westley, H., Olin, J.S., 1984. Provenance and technical studies of Mexican majolica using elemental and phase analysis. In: *Archaeological Chemistry III Adv. in Chem. Series* (ed Lambert, J. L.), pp. 151-191.

Maggetti, M., 1986. Majolika aus Mexico: ein archaömetrisches Fallbeispiel. *Fortschritte der Mineralogie*, **64**(1), 87-103.

Maggetti, M., Galetti G., 1993. Die Baukeramik von Augusta Raurica - eine mineralogisch-chemisch-technische Untersuchung. *Jahresberichte aus Augst und Kaiseraugst*, **14**, 199-225.

Maggetti, M., Galetti, G., 1994. 400 years of Galloroman ceramic production at Augusta Rauricorum, Switzerland. *Archaeometry 94 - Proceedings of the 29th International Symposium on Archaeometry, Ankara 9-14 May 1994*, 203-208.

Maggetti, M., Galetti, G., 2001. Chemical compositions of the Latin ceramics from Geneva. *Personal communication, work in progress. Data also available at the following web addresses: http://www.unifr.ch/mineral/Arch0.html and http://www.unifr.ch/mineral/referencegr/suisschem/ch1.html*

Meyer-Freuler, C., 1998. Vindonissa Feuerwehrmagazin. In: *Veröffentlichungen der Gesellschaft pro-Vindonissa*, pp. 311.

Neff, H., 1994. RQ-mode PCA of ceramic compositional data. *Archaeometry*(36), 115-130.

Nungässer, W., Maggetti, M., 1978. Mineralogisch-petrographische Untersuchung neolitischer Töpferware von Burgächisee. *Bulletin Societé Fribourgeoise de Sciences Naturelles*, **2**(67), 152-173.

Peacock, D. P. S., 1982. *Pottery in the roman world: an ethnoarchaeological approach*.

Peters, T., 1969. Mineralogische Untersuchungen an einigen schweizerischen Ziegeleirohstoffen. *Schweizerische Mineralogische Petrographische Mitteilungen*, **49**(2), 391-405.

Pettijohn, F. J., Potter, P.E., Siever, R., 1987. *Sand and Sandstone*. Springer-Verlag.

Picon, M., 1984. Le traitement des données d'analyse. *PACT*(10), 379-399.

Potts, P. J. e. a., 1995. *Microprobe techniques in the Earth Sciences*. Blackwell Sciences

Primas, M., Della Casa, P., Schmid-Sikimic, B., 1992. Archäologie zwischen Vierwaldstättersee und Gotthard. *Universität Forschungen zur prähistorischen Archäologie*, **12**. Zuerich.

Riccardi, M. P., Messiga, B., Dominuco, P., 1999. An approach to the dynamics of clay firing. *Applied Clay Science*, **15**, 393-409.

Rock, N. M. S., 1988. *Numerical Geology*. Springer-Verlag.

Schneider, G., Burmester, A., Goedicke, C., Hennicke, H.W., Kleinmann, B., Knoll, H., Maggetti, M., Rottländer, R., 1989. Naturwissenschaftliche Kriterien und Verfahren zur Beschreibung von Keramik. *Acta Praehistorica et Archaeologica* (21), 7-38.

Schneider, G., Sommer, C., (2001). Chemical composition of the stamped tiles of the 11th legion fromRottweil. *Personal communication, work in progress.*

Schubert, P., 1986. Petrographic modal analysis - a necessary complement to chemical analysis of ceramic coarse ware. *Archaeometry*, **28**(2), 163-178.

Shepard, A. O., 1976. *Ceramics for the Archaeologist*. Carnegie Institution of Washington.

Shirley, E. A. M., 1996. The building of the legionary fortress at Inchtuthil. *Britannia* (27), 111-128.

Steinby, M., 1978. Lateres signati ostienses. *Acta Instituti Romani Finlandiae*, **VII**.

Swan, A. R. H., Sandilands, M., 1995. *Introduction to Geological Data Analysis*. Blackwell Science.

Tite, M.S., 1995. Firing temperature determinations – How and why? *KWHAA Konferenser,* **34**, 37-42.

Withbread, I. K., 1986. The characterization of argillaceous inclusions in ceramic thin sections. *Archaeometry*, **28**(1), 79-88.

Wolf, S., 1999. The bricks from St. Urban: analytical and technical investigation on Cistercian bricks in Switzerland, Abstract. *Abstract book of the 179. Jahresversammlung der SANW in Luzern, 15 October 1999.*

ROEMISCHE DACHZIEGEL VON VINDONISSA

aufgenommen bis Mai 1911 und gezeichnet von Victor Jahn, Brugg. Vergl. Anzeiger f. Schw. AK 1909. 2 H. 111-119.

N⁰ 9. XXI Leg. Silbe LEG.

9a

Kurze, gedrungte Sch.

9b₁

9b₂

9b₃

N⁰ 3 L. XXI mit d. fragl. Zusatz S. C VI

vertiefte Lettern n. 3 u. 9.

3e

3f

Je und Jf sind kurze Typen mit engem VI, die XX hinken.

XXI. LEGION

Die Stempel der XXI-Legion stammen aus dem 3 ten Viertel des 1 Jahrhunderts

Die Vindonisser Ziegel tragen meist d. Beinamen d. XXI. Legion: Rapax

N⁰ 11 erh.

11

3a₁

3a₂

Typ. 3a und Typ. 3b. Die 3 Funkte liegen nicht in gerader Linie zwischen I S C. Diese Partie ist in Typ. 3a enger, Netteler und weiter im Cabes in Typ. 3b.

3b₁

3b₂

3b₃

54

Annexe A: the original Jahn's tables (1911) providing a classification of the Vindonissa tile stamps

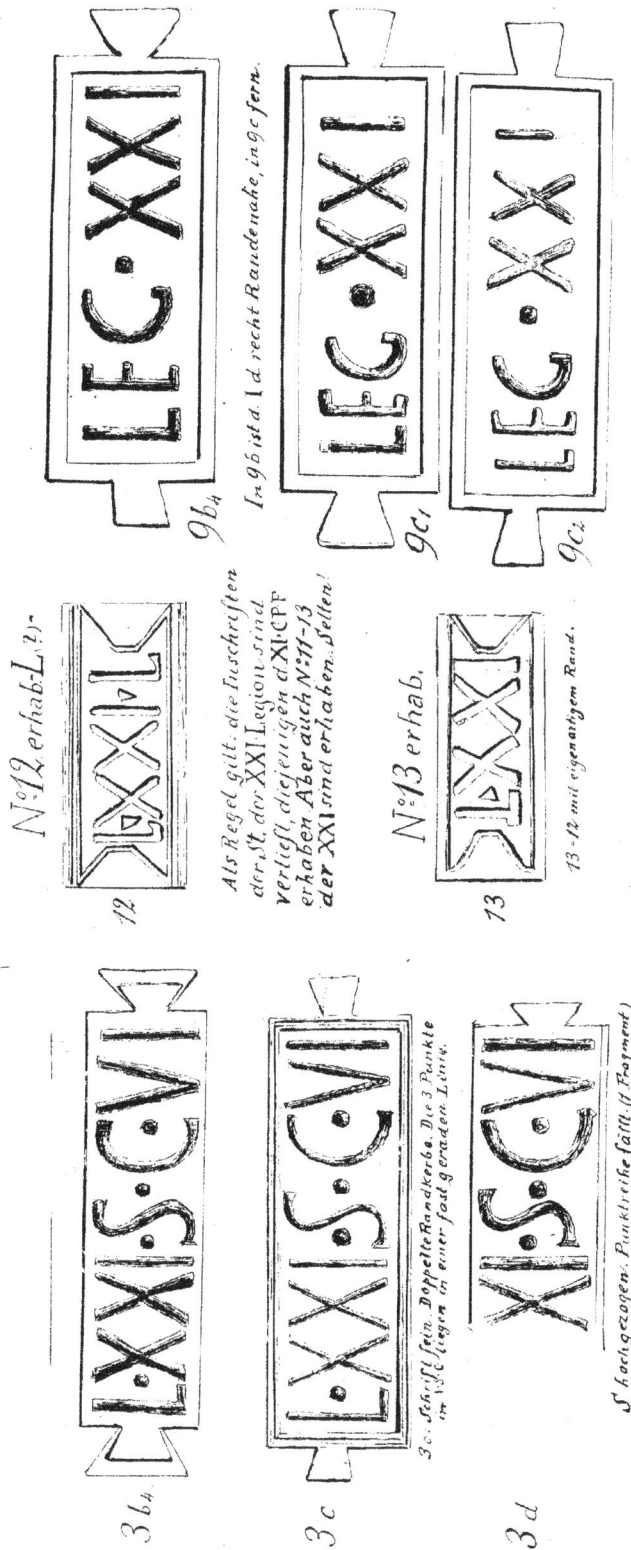

55

Annexe A: the original Jahn's tables (1911) providing a classification of the Vindonissa tile stamps

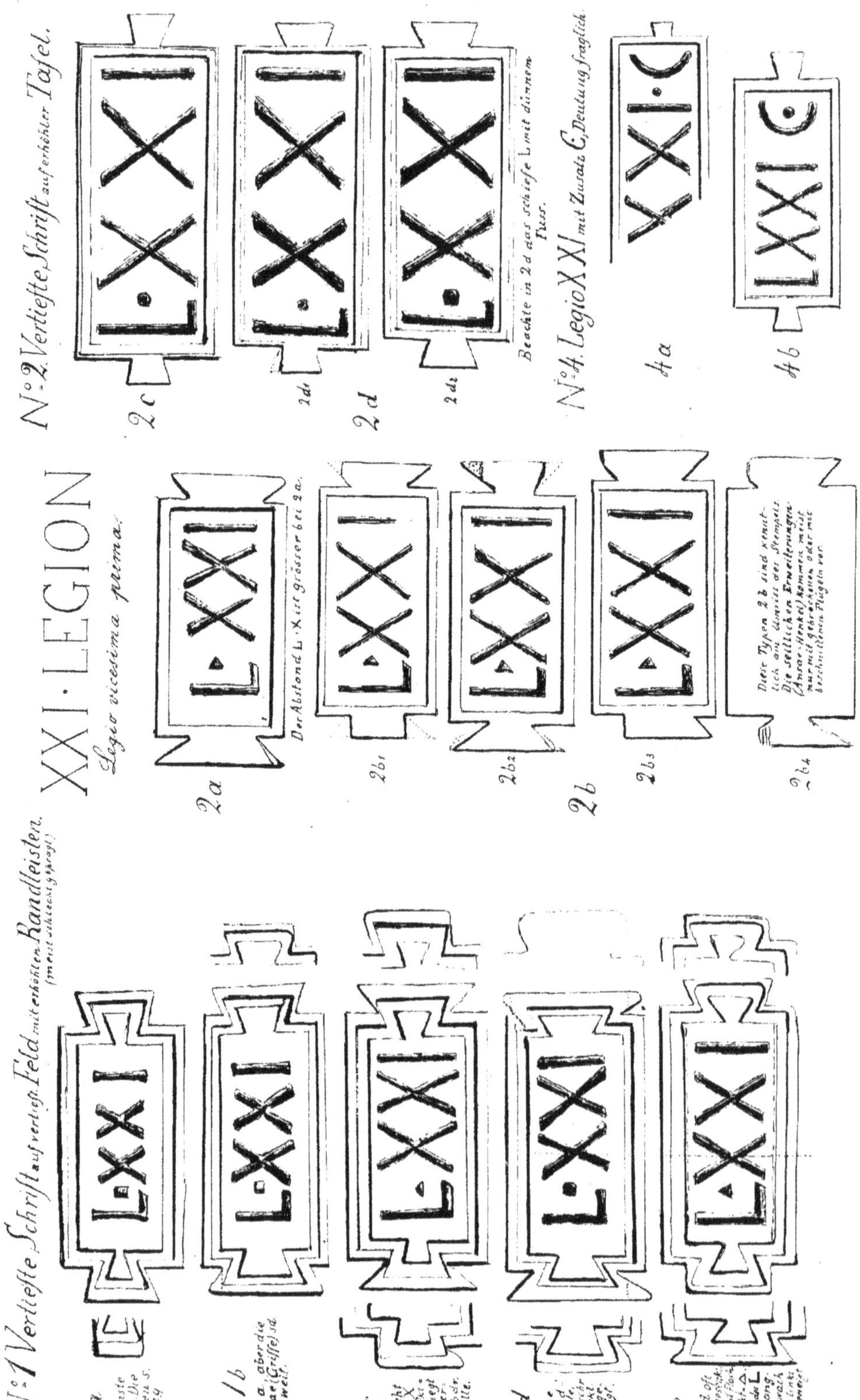

Annexe A: the original Jahn's tables (1911) providing a classification of the Vindonissa tile stamps

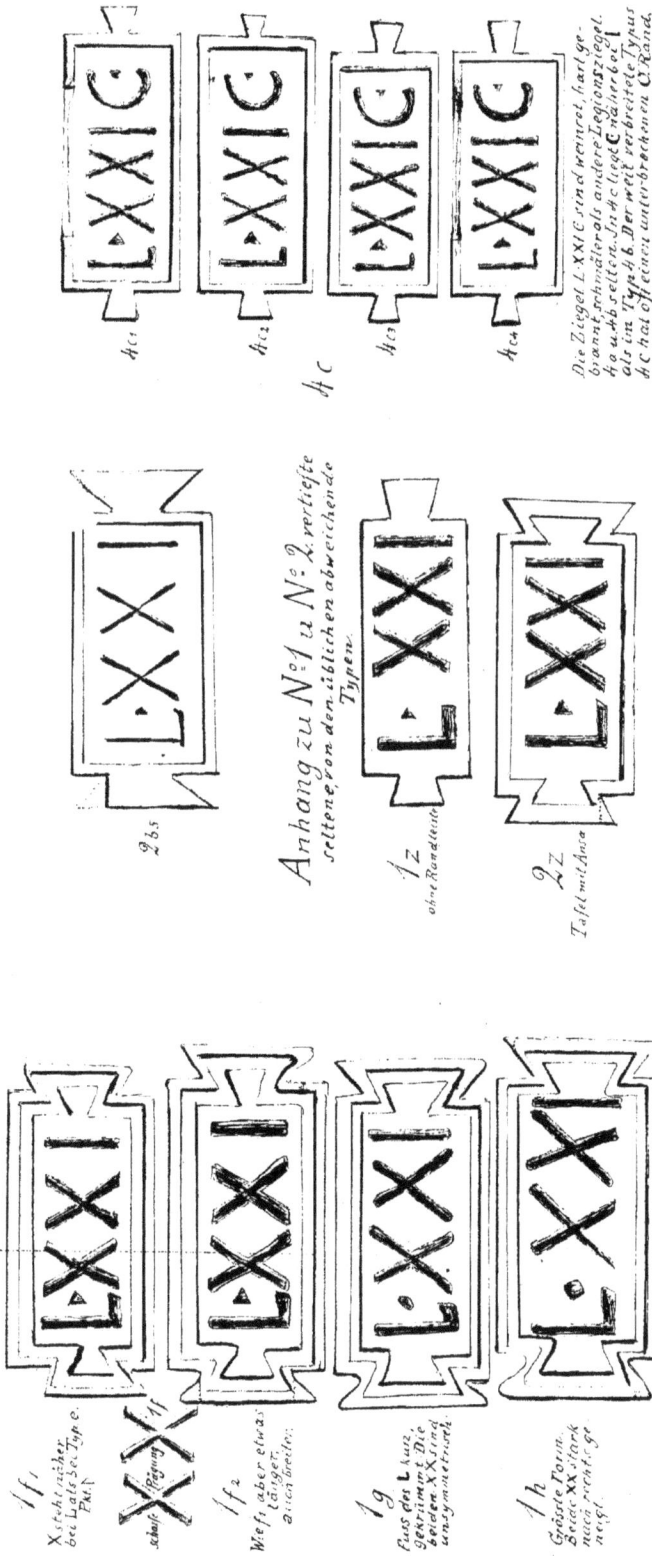

Annexe A: the original Jahn's tables (1911) providing a classification of the Vindonissa tile stamps

Annexe A: the original Jahn's tables (1911) providing a classification of the Vindonissa tile stamps

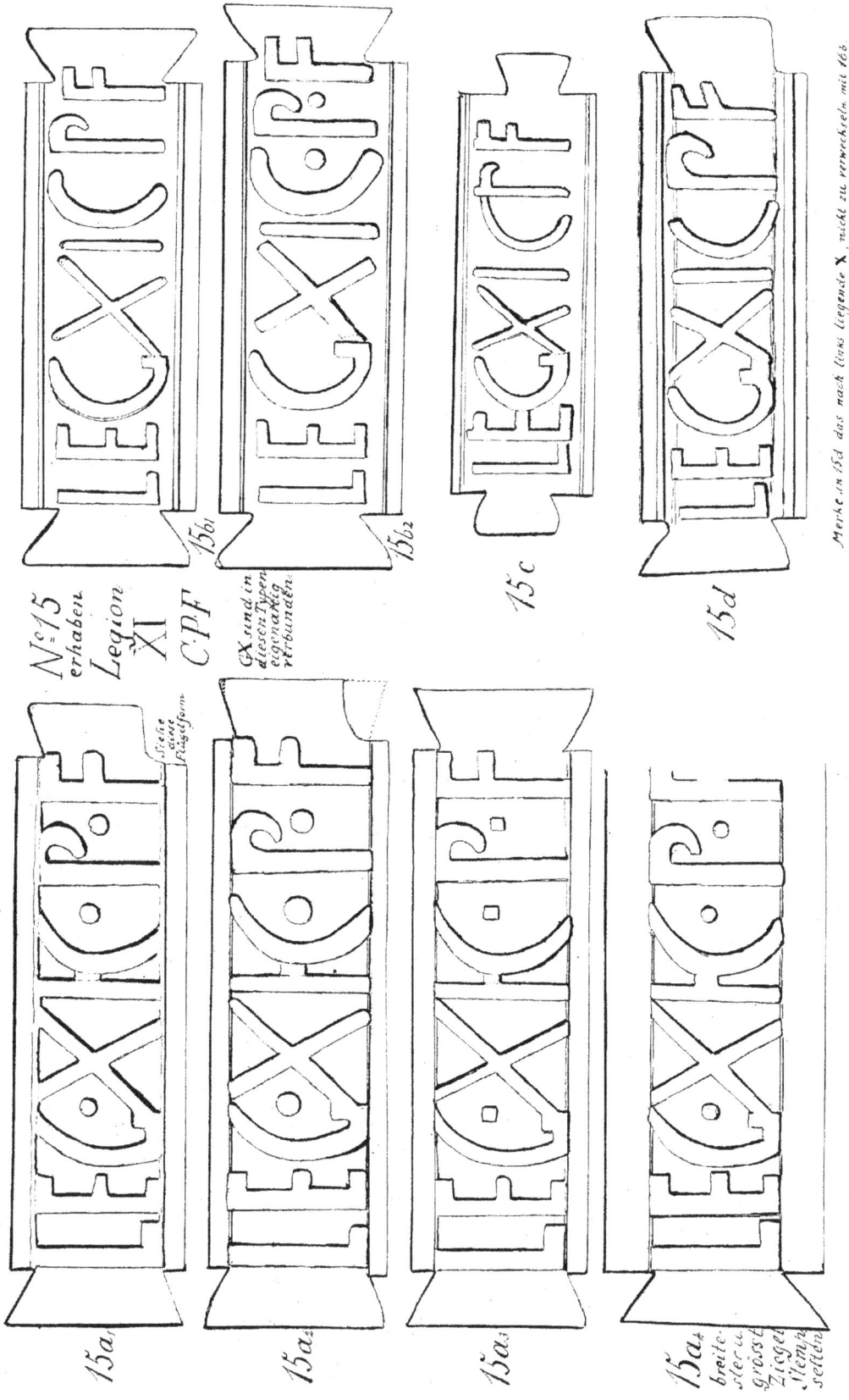

59

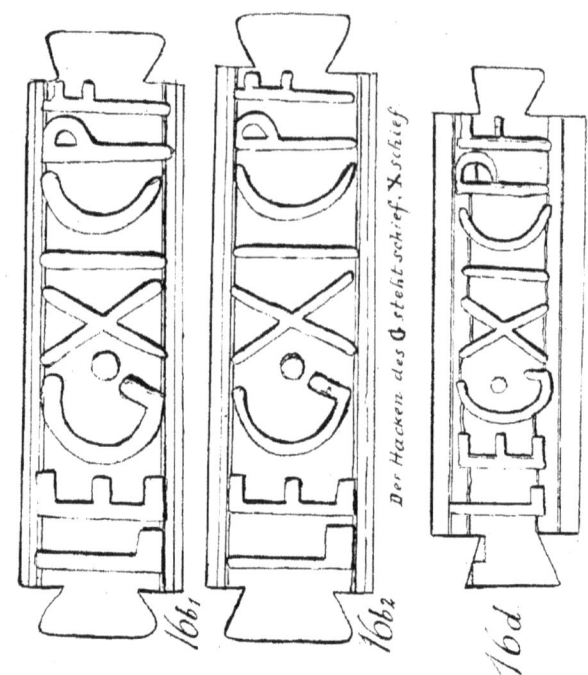

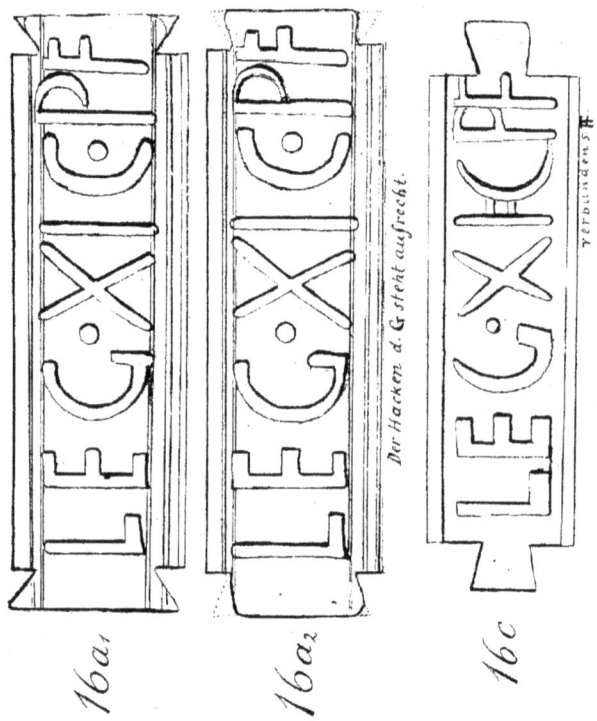

Die Kohorten-Stempel stammen aus der 2.ten Hälfte des ersten Jahrhunderts n.Ch. Sie sind selten besonders N°6 u.7.

8. Cohors vicesima sexta (civium voluntariorum Romanorum) XXVL Kohorte der Freiwilligen aus der römischen Bürgerschaft.

10 Cohors tertia Hispanorum · III. spanische Kohorte.

N° 10.

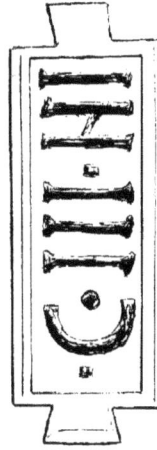

10a

10b

N° 6.

6

N° 7.

7

N° 8.

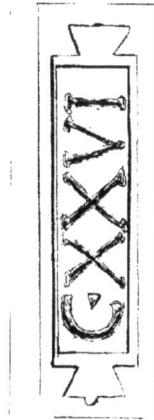

8

KOHORTEN

Den Legionen beigeordnete Hilfstruppen (Auxilia).
Alle Kohorten-Stempel sind vertieft. —

5 Cohors sexta Raetorum · VI raetische Kohorte

6-7 Cohors septima Raetorum III. raetische Koh.

N° 5.

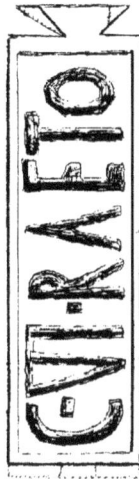

5a

5b

In Typ. 5a steht VI näher bei R als in Typus 5b.

Annexe B: Methods

B.1 Sampling

Before sampling, the surface of the object was cleaned off by sawing. This was made to eliminate the possible surface alterations due to burial and so to limit the sampling to the inner portions of the objects, which are commonly fresh and not affected by alteration.

Each ceramic specimen has been divided into four different samples:

- 20 to 100g of material, were powdered and successively used for chemical and mineralogical analyses;

- one or two little cubes (about 1 cm^3) were cut to perform porosimetric analyses;

- one parallelepiped of about 4x2x1 cm was used to prepare the petrographic thin sections

- a little piece was then conserved as hand sample.

For a small number of tiles, it was not possible to collect large specimen, so that it was necessary to take just the minimum quantity necessary for chemical analyses. This is the case for the three samples from Strasbourg.

B.2 Semi-quantitative analyses on ceramics

B.2.1. Petrography

On 26 representative samples, point counting analyses were carried out to obtain an accurate definition of their modal composition. If the dimensions of the thin section did allow it, at least 1500 counts on each section have been made. The average surface of a thin section is about 6 cm^2.

The classification of argillaceous inclusions was made following Whitbread (1986).

During point counting analyses we distinguished the clay matrix from the argillaceous rock fragments (ARF), the non plastic inclusions (Whitbread, 1986) and the pores. An arbitrary limit at 0.02 mm was defined to separate what I interpreted as clay matrix (<0.02mm), from non plastic inclusions and ARFs (>0.02mm). Finally, all the components under 1% by volume were considered accessory phases. The porosity value obtained by point counting is an important factor to discriminate different fabric, but is not representative of the real, open porosity. In fact, the porosity values obtained with this method (microscopic porosity) are much smaller than those obtained by the Hg-porosimeter, simply because of the different sensibility of the two techniques.

Petrographic analyses on the clays were performed on thin sections obtained from clay-briquettes of 8x4x1.5 cm. From each clay sample, six briquettes were obtained and fired at different temperatures between 500 and 1000°C (steps of 100°C between two successive briquettes of the same series). This technique permits to reproduce textures that are analogous to those of the ceramics studied: this allows the comparison between raw materials and final products. Classification schemes for the clays are taken from Adams et al. (1988).

B.2.2 Mineralogy

X-ray diffraction analyses were run on representative samples to define qualitatively the mineralogy of the clay matrix and, if possible, the firing-induced assemblages. As described in chapter 2, the firing-induced assemblages are important for the firing temperature estimation and were determined both on bulk analyses (mainly on the phyllosilicates peaks),and also successfully on microdomains of the samples. Ca-rich inclusions (i.e. limestone fragments) in the ceramic bodies are the most important microdomains where new phases may develop during firing of the clay (Maggetti, 1986). Analyses on such microdomains were executed by carefully separating them from the clay matrix and by analysing the powder on a Si-crystal. The separation from the ceramic bodies avoids the dilution effect of bulk analyses, whereas the use of the Si-crystal as support of the powder decreases the intensity of the background of the X-ray spectrum.

I based the estimate of the maximum temperature attained by the sample, on previous experimental works on calcareous and not calcareous clays (Maggetti and Heimann, 1979; Jornet, 1980; Maggetti, 1986; Dominuco et al., 1998; Riccardi et al., 1999).

X-ray diffraction analyses were performed at the Institute of Mineralogy, University of Fribourg using a Philips PW1800 Diffractometer at the following operating conditions:

- Cu Kα, λ= 1.541828 Å;

- 40 mA current;

- 40 kV voltage;

- 2θ varying from 2° to 65° (or 70°);

- step angles 0.02° or 0.01° 2θ;

- measuring time 1 or 2 s/step

B.3 Geochemistry

B.3.1 Sample preparation

Analyses were performed on glassy tablets for both major and trace elements. Calibration of major and trace elements was made on 59 standards.

Glassy tablets were prepared by starting with about 3 g of powdered sample dried for 6-8 hours at 110°C and fired at 1000°C for 1 hour. Samples were weighted after each step in order to calculate the loss on ignition (LOI).

0.700 g of calcined powder was then mixed with 0.350g of Li fluoride and 6.650g of Li tetraborate, put into a Pt crucible and melted at 1150°C for 10 min. using a PHILIPS PERL'X-2 machine.

B.3.2. Measurements

Major elements (Si, Ti, Al, Fe, Mn, Mg, Ca, Na, K, P) and trace elements (Ba, Cr, Cu, Nb, Ni, Pb, Rb, Sr, Y, V, Zn) of 203 samples were analysed at the Institute of Mineralogy, University of Fribourg using X-ray fluorescence (XRF).

Analytical reproducibility and detection limits for major and trace elements after standard analyses are reported in table B.1.

	AR (wt%)	DL (wt%)		AR (ppm)	DL (ppm)
SiO_2	0.25	0.01	Ba	20	12
TiO_2	0.01	0.01	Cr	5	5
Al_2O_3	0.08	0.01	Cu	4	4
Fe_2O_3T	0.05	0.01	Nb	2	2
MnO	-	0.01	Ni	3	3
MgO	0.02	0.01	Pb	4	7
CaO	0.05	0.01	Rb	3	3
Na_2O	0.02	0.01	Sr	4	3
K_2O	0.02	0.01	V	6	5
P_2O_5	0.01	0.01	Y	3	3
			Zn	4	3

Table B.1: XRF analytical reproducibility and detection limits after standard analyses for the measured elements. Fe_2O_3T: total iron measured as Fe^{3+}

On five randomly selected samples, two analyses were executed by separately powdering two different specimen. This was done to test the sample reproducibility. If the object is not homogeneous, the small quantity of sampled material could produce analytical results not representative of the sample and with reduced precision. The largest variation between two specimens of one same object were observed for P and Mn. For Mn the variation may be as high as 7 %; this could be explained by the very low amounts of MnO, which are always near the limit of detection. The variations of the other elements are generally below 1 % and rarely reach 1.5 %. Just in the case of sample FG49 the variation for CaO is 5.13 % between the two specimens. Generally it was possible to observe that the sample reproducibility was rather good, since the differences among two specimens of the same samples were not significant if compared to the differences observed between groups of samples (Table B.2).

B.3.3 Contamination problems

Contamination of archaeological objects is often a major problem, when dealing with their chemical composition. The long burial and the circulation of fluids in the soil may alter strongly the original composition of the ceramics. Some mobile elements like K and Na, are easily leached from the percolating solutions and others, like Ca and Ba may be fixed in the sherd by precipitation processes. For this reason, it is common to remove the surface of archaeological specimens before the analysis to eliminate the contribution of the most external and presumably altered portion. A control over the amount of contamination in a specimen may be made in a quantitative way on the chemical analyses and in a semi-quantitative way on the petrographic thin section.

Phosphor is considered an element whose concentration may be strongly affected by the contamination. Phosphor in natural clays is commonly present in concentrations of 0.1-0.5% as P_2O_5 percent weight (Koritnig, 1978, cited in Bearat and Dufournier 1994). An increase in P_2O_5 over 0.5% is commonly explained as due to contamination processes, but the increase may be justified in two different ways. Bearat and Dufournier (1994) assert that an augmentation in P_2O_5 in the ceramics, especially pottery, may be induced by their original use. The use of pottery as holders for P-rich substances (milk, wine...) is often at the base of an enrichment in this element, because of fixation of phosphor-rich compounds inthe pores or of P in the structure of clay minerals.

Lemoine and Picon (1981) state that an increase of P in the ceramics may relate to leaching of other, more mobile elements (K, Na, Si, Mg) during burial and should not derive from an external source. In a suite of archaeological samples, a negative correlation between mobile elements and P for the sample with anomalous P_2O_5 contents, could be the evidence of contamination (leaching of some elements and relative enrichment in others, which are more stable to the alteration processes).

Since in this study we are dealing with roof tiles, I will not consider the hypothesis of Bearat and Dufournier

	FG 76-1	FG 76-2	Abs(% var)	FG 58-1	FG 58-2	Abs(% var)	FG 62-1	FG 62-2
SiO_2	68.64	68.85	0.3	60.02	60.23	0.3	68.53	68.52
TiO_2	0.71	0.71	-	0.75	0.76	1.3	0.67	0.67
Al_2O_3	15.55	15.55	-	16.84	16.83	0.1	14.95	15.02
Fe_2O_{3T}	5.88	5.88	-	6.6	6.56	0.6	5.54	5.56
MnO	0.13	0.13	-	0.15	0.15	-	0.12	0.12
MgO	2.39	2.38	0.4	4.24	4.23	0.2	2.34	2.37
CaO	1.04	1.05	1.0	5.73	5.7	0.5	2.2	2.18
Na_2O	1.6	1.59	0.6	1.26	1.27	0.8	1.55	1.56
K_2O	3.57	3.58	0.3	3.67	3.62	1.4	3.44	3.45
P_2O_5	0.11	0.12	8.7	0.4	0.38	5.1	0.15	0.16
SUM	99.62	99.84	0.2	99.66	99.73	0.1	99.49	99.61
Ba	355	354	0.3	412	412	-	369	393
Cr	133	131	1.5	152	152	-	128	126
Nb	11	9	20	15	12	22.2	13	12
Ni	89	84	5.8	102	104	1.9	88	88
Rb	146	147	0.7	141	141	-	145	142
Sr	57	57	-	103	102	1.0	79	79
V	80	86	7.2	70	73	4.2	91	89
Y	33	33	-	39	38	2.6	34	37
Zn	64	177	93.8	84	81	3.6	106	61

	FG 49-1	FG 49-2	Abs(% var)	FG 15-1	FG 15-2	Abs(% var)
SiO_2	70.51	70.49	-	64.81	65.07	0.4
TiO_2	0.65	0.65	-	0.75	0.75	-
Al_2O_3	15.1	15.19	0.6	16.88	16.86	0.1
Fe_2O_{3T}	5.16	5.21	1.0	6.69	6.65	0.6
MnO	0.13	0.14	7.4	0.16	0.15	6.5
MgO	2.04	2.07	1.5	2.97	2.96	0.3
CaO	1.2	1.14	5.1	1.92		1.1
Na_2O	1.36	1.4	2.9	1.48	1.49	0.7
K_2O	3.49	3.46	0.9	4.06	4.04	0.5
P_2O_5	0.09	0.09	-	0.18	0.21	15.4
SUM	99.73	99.84	0.1	99.91	100.07	0.2
Ba	451	468	3.7	401	422	5.1
Cr	96	98	2.1	137	139	1.5
Nb	16	15	6.5	15	15	-
Ni	71	71	-	104	99	4.9
Rb	137	138	0.7	180	177	1.7
Sr	78	77	1.3	78	77	1.3
V	93	98	5.2	99	97	2.0
Y	35	34	2.9	38	37	2.7
Zn	67	63	6.2	98	95	3.1

Table B.2: Sample reproducibility after XRF chemical analyses performed on pairs of specimens from 5 randomly selected samples. The absolute percent variation of each element for each pair of analyses is reported

(1994); that of Lemoine and Picon (1982) seems to be the most appropriate in our case.

We considered samples with P_2O_5 contents >0.5 wt% as potentially contaminated. In these cases, each chemical element was recalculated to balance the contamination effect, by the following equation:

$$X_a' = (X_a * 100) / (Total - P_2O_5^*)$$

where,

X_a' :   recalculated value for the element a

X_a :   measured value for the element a

Total: sum of the weight percent for all the measured elements

$P_2O_5^*$: weight percent of the measured P_2O_5 reduced by the average P_2O_5 for all other samples

This calculation does not take into account the possibility that elements like Ca and Ba may be fixed from an external source into a contaminated ceramic sample. This eventuality can be checked by the observation of the chemical results (anomalous high Ba contents) and by the observation of petrographic thin sections. In thin section it is commonly possible to observe the precipitation of secondary phases (carbonates, sulphates, etc.) into the pores of the ceramic bodies. The amount of these concretions may be modally estimated and give a semi-quantitative evaluation of the alteration and an idea of the involved processes. Following these considerations, before the interpretation of our data, I always evaluated the possibility of sample contamination.

For the sample FG57, which looked to be one of the most alte ed on the surface (white crusts and concretions, ceramic body badly preserved and soft), I performed two chemical analyses on two different fractions of the same sample. I first removed two to three millimetres from the surface and analysed this fraction. A second chemical analysis was carried out on the core of the sample. The results of the analyses (table B.3) demonstrate that the surface is enriched in P_2O_5 , CaO and MnO and slightly depleted in K_2O, Na_2O and SiO_2. The concentrations of K and Na show respectively a relative depletion of 4 and

2% on the surface, whereas CaO and P_2O_5 show relative increases of 12 and 37% respectively. Although the relative variations seem quite important, they have scarce influence on the global analytical result (CaO increases from 1.05 to 1.19%).

The influence of burial seems to be important, even if not dramatic, only for the most external part of the sample. Two to three millimetres inside, the composition does not display evidences of leaching or re-deposition of elements.

B.4 Statistics

A detailed review of statistical analysis in archaeometry is beyond the scope of this work: in this paragraph, I will discuss the main techniques used, and the analysis procedures. All analyses were carried out with the SPSS 10 package.

B.4.1 Principal Component Analysis: method and procedures

Principal Component Analysis (PCA) was performed on the data set of the chemical composition of samples to verify whether the population had an internal structure and to validate the information collected through bivariate chemical plots and petrographic analyses.

The PCA allows to obtain a simplified representation (two or three dimensions) of complex, n-dimensional data (Baxter, 1994). A table of chemical compositions of p archaeological specimens, for which n elements were measured, typically represents such a complex data set. A Principal Component (PC) extracted during the analysis, is a linear combination of the original variable. If we deal with chemical composition a PC of the original data matrix will have the form:

$$P_x = a_1 Al_2O_3 + a_2 MgO + ... + a_n Cr$$

Where a_1, a_2, ..., a_n, are coefficients whose values are determined in a way that:

1.   the data plotted on the first component P_1 has the highest variance

2.   the first two components (P_1 and P_2) are uncorrelated, and

3.   the spread on the second component is the second greatest possible,

4.   and so on for the further n components.

A successful PCA should reduce the dimensionality of a multivariate space to three to four principal components, which may explain 80-90% of the total variation of the data set. This means that the picture obtained from the first PCs does not represent the reality, but a very good approximation of it.

Compound	FG57 surface (wt%)	FG57 core (wt%)	Relative variation (%)	Element	FG57 surface (ppm)	FG57 core (ppm)	Relative variation (%)
SiO_2	71.07	71.47	-0.6	Ba	462	436	5.8
TiO_2	0.77	0.76	1.3	Cr	109	104	4.7
Al_2O_3	14.64	14.79	-1	Cu	4	4	-
Fe_2O_{3T}	5.57	5.42	2.7	Nb	16	19	-17.1
MnO	0.12	0.08	40	Ni	66	66	-
MgO	1.5	1.55	-3.3	Pb	42	38	10
CaO	1.19	1.05	12.5	Rb	111	120	-7.8
Na_2O	1.48	1.51	-2	Sr	94	80	16.1
K_2O	2.54	2.64	-3.9	V	66	68	-3
P_2O_5	0.7	0.48	37.3	Y	40	38	5.1
SUM	99.58	99.75	-	Zn	86	170	-65.6

Table B.3: Chemical composition of two specimen from the same sample. showing changes in composition between the fresh core and the weathered surface of the sample.

In the calculation SiO_2, P_2O_5, Cu, Pb and Zn were not considered in the variable set. SiO_2 was removed because it is always strongly correlated with Al_2O_3 and because it is the dominant oxide, accounting for about 60-80% of the composition of the ceramics. As suggested by Rock (1988), strongly correlated variables of a closed data set, such as chemical analyses are, may strongly influence the structure of the result. P_2O_5 was discarded because its concentration can be strongly affected by contamination. Cu was not considered because its measured concentration in a large number of samples was below the detection limit of the instrument (5 ppm). I then discarded Pb because the variations from sample to sample had commonly no significance. Finally, in some repeated chemical analyses Zn contents were not reproducible, therefore Zn was eliminated from dataset too.

Statistical results are strongly conditioned from the internal variance of each variable. The presence of variables expressed on different scales (in our case Wt.% and ppm) may condition the analysis in a strong and not always desirable way. Some transformations are necessary to avoid scale-related problems. Following Baxter (1994), the data matrix was transformed to a new one by the following equation:

$$Y_{Mg} = \ln(X_{Mg}), \quad (1)$$

where X_{Mg} is the original value, say for magnesium. The logarithmic transformation solves the problems related to the occurrence of not normal distribution of the data, but can result in some variables (for example those near to zero) having a large influence on the analysis (Baxter, 1994). For this reason a series of analyses with another logarithmic transformation was tested, with the form:

$$Y_{Mg} = \ln(X_{Mg}+1) \quad (2)$$

no significant change in the analyses results was observed, the transformation (1) was used.

The SPSS package standardises, as default, the data matrix as follow:

$$Z_{Mg} = (Y_{Mg} - Y^m{}_{Mg})/ sY_{Mg} \quad ,$$

where Y^m is the average Y value, and sY is the Y standard deviation.

This standardisation reduces the ln-transformed variables into new ones with equal variance and zero means. This transformation further improves the bell-shaped distribution of the data.

Eigenvalues were extracted from the correlation matrix with a cut-off value of 1 as suggested by Baxter (1994). In this way the three first principal components always explained a variation greater than 75%. A cut-off values of 0.7, as suggested in Jolliffe (1986), resulted in too many PC extracted with no significant increase of the total variance explained.

B.4.2 Discriminant Analysis, method and procedures

Using the same variable set of PCA, a first Discriminant Analysis (DA) was carried out on a selected number of samples with very well characterised fabrics and chemical compositions. This allowed to build well constrained groups of samples that were compared with all the samples having uncertain fabrics or chemical composition.

DA is in fact a statistical tool that need some assumptions before starting and then runs in steps.

First, the operator has to define a sub-set of data, belonging to one or more groups (Baxter, 1994). The grouping should not be made strictly on the same variables, which are going to be used for Discriminant Analysis (Rock, 1988). In our case, the groups were constructed conjugating archaeological, petrographic and chemical observations.

The first step in DA, the discrimination, finds functions maximising the differences between the pre-defined groups and minimising the internal scatter within each group. The second step, the classification, allocates unknown objects to the defined groups, as a function of their characteristics. The probability that a sample belongs to a group is expressed as the squared distance of the unclassified sample (Mahalanobis' distance) from the group centre (centroid).

Picon (1984) states that, if maximum and minimum values of the squared Mahalanobis distances (D^2) for each defined group of sample are considered, the probability that an unknown sample belongs to that group may be postulated as follows:

- If the sample has D^2 close to the group minimum, it has good probabilities to belong to the group.

- If the sample has D^2 close to the group maximum, or even greater, it has few or none probability to belong to the group.

Discriminant analyses were carried out on the transformed data matrix, consisting of a selected number of samples, separated into chemo-petrographic groups. In the linear procedure, all variables are entered together and the discriminant functions are calculated on the basis of the whole set of variables. After the "training" phase, in which the validity of the groups was proved, I ran a series of DA by adding each "unknown" sample and trying to classify each of them in a group.

B.5 Porosimetry

Mercury-pressure porosimetry analyses were performed on 104 representative sample. Analyses were carried out on little specimens (about 1g) with a Micromeritics Autopore II 9215 at the Institute of Mineralogy, University of Fribourg. Mercury porosimetry is based on the capillary law, which rules the liquid penetration into small pores. Ideal penetration of a non-wetting liquid like mercury, into cylindrical pores is expressed by Washburn's equation:

$$D = -(1/P)2 \, \gamma \cos\theta$$

where D is the pore diameter, P the applied pressure, γ the surface tension and θ the wetting angle. The volume (V) of intruded mercury is measured directly as a function of the applied pressure.

In the case of ceramics, pores are rarely cylindrical, but the above equation is generally accepted as a good model to approximate the reality.

B.6 Technical tests

To compare the technical properties of the archaeological tiles with those of the modern products, standard quality tests were executed on a restricted number of tile specimens. Because of the large quantity of material required for these texts, it was only possible to perform the analyses on 10 specimens. The tests of the resistance to flexure and to freezing conditions were executed with the technical support of the laboratories at the tile factory Zürcher Zigeleien Wancor.

The resistance to 3-point flexure F is measured by putting a 11-12 cm long and about 4 cm wide ceramic specimen on a support made of two steel knives. The space between the knives is 10 cm. A third knife exercises an increasing pressure in the middle of the specimen. The pressure P at which the specimen breaks (breaking load) is measured and the resistance to flexure is calculated as follows:

$$F(\text{N/mm}^2) = 1.5(P*d)/(w*t),$$

where d is the distance between the knives, and w and t represent the width and the thickness of the specimen, respectively. All distances are expressed in mm.

Following the actual normative, the tiles must resist a breaking load of at least 1000 N and the resistance to flexure value must be at least 12 N/mm² (reference European norms UNI EN 8635/13).

The resistance to freezing conditions consists in exposing the specimen to alternate cycles of freezing and thawing under wet conditions. One cycle consists of:

-90 min. exposition of a wet specimen to a temperature of −15°C

-48 min. of simulated rain at +10°C

To be conformable to the actual norms (reference European norms, UNI EN 8635/11), a specimen has to withstand 150 cycles without damages (fissures, cracks, etc.)

B7. Mineral chemistry

Analyses with the electron microprobe were carried out to characterise the crystal chemistry of major and accessory phases. WDS analyses were performed at the Institute of Mineralogy and Petrography, University of Bern, with a Cameca SX-50 equipped with four X-ray spectrometers. Operating conditions were 15 kV acceleration, 20nA current, 20sec counting time for each element plus 5sec for the background. Beam spot size ranged between 2 and 10 μm: large spots were used on alkali-rich phases, such as feldspars or micas to avoid overheat-induced diffusion of light-elements.

X-ray intensities were automatically corrected to oxide-percent concentration by the ZAF correction procedure provided by Cameca. Counting errors after standard analyses (3σ) are less than 4% for Na and K, and less than 2% for Si, Al, Ti, Ca, Mg, Fe, Mn, and Cr. Analytical precision is better than 3% for Na and K and better than 1% for all other elements.

Annexe C: List of the samples ordered in function of their archaeological site of provenance.

Archeological site of provenance	Analysis n°	Type of object	Stamp-type (Jahn, 1909)	Type of inscription (*Tegulae*) or decoration (*Antefixa*)	Notes	Inventory n°
ALPNACH	FGI61	*Tegula*	2	LXXI		A-A1Z10
ALPNACH	FGI62	*Tegula*	4	LXXIC		A-A1Z19
ALPNACH	FGI63	*Tegula*	15A	LEGXICPF		A-A1Z29
ALPNACH	FGI64	*Tegula*	15	LEGXICPF		A-A1Z41
ALPNACH	FGI65	*Tegula*	1	LXXI		A-A1Z1
ALPNACH	FGI66	*Tegula*	2 C/D	LXXI		A-A1Z12
ALPNACH	FGI67	*Tegula*	2 C/D	LXXI		A-A1Z7
ALPNACH	FGI68	*Tegula*	9	LEGXXI		A-A1Z24
ALPNACH	FGI69	*Tegula*	16 A	LEGXICPF		A-A1Z38
ALPNACH	FGI70	*Tegula*	14	LEGXICPF		A-A1Z34
ALPNACH	FGI71	*Tegula*	14 F2	LEGXICPF		A-A1Z48
ALPNACH	FGI72	*Tegula*	3	LXXISCVI		A-A1Z16
ALPNACH	FGI73	*Tegula*	3	LXXISCVI		A-A1Z22
AVENCHES	FGI45	*Tegula*	4	LXXIC	damaged stamp*	67-13262
AVENCHES	FGI46	*Tegula*	4	LXXIC	damaged stamp*	62-3081
AVENCHES	FGI47	*Tegula*	4	LXXIC		1946-129A
AVENCHES	FGI48	*Tegula*	4	LXXIC	damaged stamp*	1866-1289
AVENCHES	FGI49	*Tegula*	4	LXXIC	damaged stamp*	4752 78-787
AVENCHES	FGI50	*Tegula*	3	LXXISCVI		4351
AVENCHES	FGI51	*Tegula*	4	LXXIC	damaged stamp*	1902-3307
AVENCHES	FGI52	*Tegula*	4	LXXIC		64-4209
AVENCHES	FGI53	*Tegula*	4	LXXIC	overfired?	1866-1290
AVENCHES	FGI54	*Tegula*	4	LXXIC	damaged stamp*	1875-1675
HAUT VULLY (Fribourg)	FGI44	*Tegula*	4	LXXIC		Ron63 532
JORESSANT (Fribourg)	FGI59	*Tegula*	4	LXXIC		FR1
KAISTEN	FG82	*Tegula*	4	LXXIC		6169
KAISTEN	FGI01	*Tegula*	3	LXXISCVI		6172
KAISTEN	FGI18	*Tegula*	14	LEGXICPF		6160
KAISTEN	FGI19	*Tegula*	3?	LXXISCVI		6162
KAISTEN	FGI20	*Tegula*	2	LXXI		6193
KAISTEN	FGI21	*Tegula*	15	LEGXICPF		6164
KAISTEN	FGI22	*Tegula*	15	LEGXICPF		6177

Annexe C: List of the samples ordered in function of their archaeological site of provenance.

Archeological site of provenance	Analysis n°	Type of object	Stamp-type (Jahn, 1909)	Type of inscription (Tegulae) or decoration (Antefixa)	Notes	Inventory n°
KAISTEN	FG123	*Tegula*	14	LEGXICPF		6180?
NEUCHATEL	FG158	*Tegula*	4	LXXIC		mar125
PETINESCA	FG155	*Tegula*	4	LXXIC		4421
PETINESCA	FG156	*Tegula*	4	LXXIC		1678-22654
PETINESCA	FG157	*Tegula*	4	LXXIC		15015-1679
ROTTWEIL	FG221	Pot	NO STAMP	-		ZV1192/20
ROTTWEIL	FG222	Pot	NO STAMP	-		1118/270
ROTTWEIL	FG223	Pot	NO STAMP			ZV 1330/99
ROTTWEIL	FG224	Pot	NO STAMP			ZW 1118/86
ROTTWEIL	FG225	Pot	NO STAMP	-		ZV1330/120
ROTTWEIL	FG232	*Tegula*		LEGXICPF	similar to Jahn 14	-
ROTTWEIL	FG237	*Tegula*		LEGXICPF	similar to Jahn 14	-
ROTTWEIL	FG238	*Tegula*		LEGXICPF	similar to Jahn 14	-
RUFENACH	FG97	*Tegula*	1	LXXI		14:383
RUPPERSWIL	FG140	*Tegula*	16	LEGXICPF	overfired	-
SEEB	FG174	*Tegula*	12	LXXIL		ZS38
SEEB	FG175	*Tegula*	13	LXXI		ZS44
SEEB	FG176	*Tegula*	12	LXXIL		ZS18
SEEB	FG177	*Tegula*	12	LXXIL		ZS39
SEEB	FG178	*Tegula*	12	LXXIL		ZS8
SEEB	FG179	*Tegula*	12	LXXIL		ZS4
SEEB	FG180	*Tegula*	12	LXXIL		ZS36
SEEB	FG181	*Tegula*	12	LXXIL		ZS42
SEEB	FG182	*Tegula*	12	LXXIL		ZS14
SEEB	FG183	*Tegula*	16D	LEGXICPF		ZS12
SEEB	FG184	*Tegula*	3C	LXXISCVI		ZS16
SEEB	FG185	*Tegula*	2C	LXXI		ZS86
SEEB	FG186	*Tegula*	3B	LXXISCVI		ZS85
SEEB	FG187	*Tegula*	2B	LXXI		ZS76
SEEB	FG188	*Tegula*	3B?	LXXISCVI		ZS80
SEEB	FG189	*Tegula*	3C	LXXISCVI		ZS66
SEEB	FG190	*Tegula*	4C	LXXIC		ZS67
SEEB	FG191	*Tegula*	3	LXXISCVI		ZS72

70

Annexe C: List of the samples ordered in function of their archaeological site of provenance.

Archeological site of provenance	Analysis n°	Type of object	Stamp-type (Jahn, 1909)	Type of inscription (*Tegulae*) or decoration (*Antefixa*)	Notes	Inventory n°
SEEB	FGI92	*Tegula*	3 (B3)	LXXISCVI	not analysed	ZS27
SEEB	FGI93	*Tegula*	2C	LXXI		ZS26
SEEB	FGI94	*Tegula*	15 A	LEGXICPF		ZS96
SEEB	FGI95	*Tegula*	16 a	LEGXICPF		ZS97
SEEB	FGI96	*Tegula*	12	LXXIL		(N°58, 1979, Schnitte 28)
SEEB	FGI97	*Tegula*	4	LXXIC		ZS60
SEEB	FGI98	*Tegula*	3 (B3)	LXXISCVI		ZS59
SEEB	FGI99	*Tegula*	2 (c/d)	LXXI		ZS63
SEEB	FG200	*Tegula*	13	LXXI		ZS30
SEEB	FG201	*Tegula*	12	LXXIL		ZS47
SEEB	FG202	*Tegula*	12	LXXIL		ZS31
SEEB	FG203	*Tegula*	13	LXXI		ZS35
SEEB	FG204	*Tegula*	12	LXXIL		ZS37
SEEB	FG205	*Tegula*	12	LXXIL		ZS34
SEEB	FG206	*Tegula*	12	LXXI		ZS28
SEEB	FG207	*Tegula*	12	LXXIL		ZS46
STRASBOURG	FG226	*Tegula*	-	LXXI Z?		8334
STRASBOURG	FG227	*Tegula*	-	?? XXI		9758
STRASBOURG	FG228	*Tegula*	-	LE XXI R ?		7547 ?
VINDONISSA	FG10	*Tegula*	1	LXXI		V76/153.3
VINDONISSA	FG11	*Tegula*	1 b	LXXI		V76/57.1
VINDONISSA	FG12	*Tegula*	2 c/d	LXXI		V76/166.19
VINDONISSA	FG13	*Tegula*	2 C	LXXI		V76/234.3
VINDONISSA	FG14	*Tegula*	3	LXXISCVI		V76/173.4
VINDONISSA	FG15	*Tegula*	3E	LXXISCVI		V76/257.1
VINDONISSA	FG16	*Tegula*	4	LXXIC		V76/25.9
VINDONISSA	FG17	*Tegula*	4	LXXIC		V76/422.11
VINDONISSA	FG18	*Tegula*	4	LXXIC	damaged stamp*	V76/40.2
VINDONISSA	FG19	*Tegula*	4	LXXIC		V76/16.1
VINDONISSA	FG20	*Tegula*	9	LEGXXI		V76/38.12
VINDONISSA	FG21	*Tegula*	9	LEGXXI		V76/51.2
VINDONISSA	FG22	*Tegula*	11	LXXI		V76/407.5
VINDONISSA	FG23	*Tegula*	12	LXXIL		V76/480.6
VINDONISSA	FG24	*Tegula*	12	LXXIL		V76/1.14

Annexe C: List of the samples ordered in function of their archaeological site of provenance.

Archeological site of provenance	Analysis n°	Type of object	Stamp-type (Jahn, 1909)	Type of inscription (*Tegulae*) or decoration (*Antefixa*)	Notes	Inventory n°
VINDONISSA	FG25	*Tegula*	12? 13?	LXXIL? LXXI?		V76/393.1
VINDONISSA	FG26	*Tegula*	14	LEGXICPF		V76/246.1
VINDONISSA	FG27	*Tegula*	14	LEGXICPF		V76/71.1
VINDONISSA	FG28	*Tegula*	15	LEGXICPF		V76/515.6
VINDONISSA	FG29	*Tegula*	15	LEGXICPF		V76/491.24
VINDONISSA	FG30	*Tegula*	16C	LEGXICPF		V76/25.3
VINDONISSA	FG31	*Tegula*	16C	LEGXICPF		V76/176.7
VINDONISSA	FG32	*Tegula*	16	LEGXICPF		V76/169.8
VINDONISSA	FG33	*Tegula*	12? 13?	LXXIL? LXXI?		V82.2/129.4
VINDONISSA	FG34	*Tegula*	5	CVI RAETO		V82.2/159.17
VINDONISSA	FG35	*Tegula*	6	CVII R		V82.2/237.26
VINDONISSA	FG36	*Tegula*	12	LXXIL		V82.2/355.8
VINDONISSA	FG37	*Tegula*	10	CIII HI		-
VINDONISSA	FG38	*Tegula*	5	CVI RAETO		28.4498
VINDONISSA	FG39	*Tegula*	8	CXXVI		59.2818
VINDONISSA	FG40	*Tegula*	7	CVII R		30.2665
VINDONISSA	FG41	*Tegula*	1E	LXXI		34.6044
VINDONISSA	FG47	*Tegula*	4	LXXIC		-
VINDONISSA	FG48	*Tegula*	4	LXXIC		-
VINDONISSA	FG49	*Tegula*	4	LXXIC		-
VINDONISSA	FG50	*Tegula*	5	CVI RAETO		-
VINDONISSA	FG51	*Tegula*	1	LXXI		27340
VINDONISSA	FG52	*Tegula*	9	LEGXXI		59.2712
VINDONISSA	FG53	*Tegula*	16	LEGXICPF		-
VINDONISSA	FG54	*Tegula*	16	LEGXICPF		26.965
VINDONISSA	FG55	*Tegula*	9	LEGXXI		37.167
VINDONISSA	FG56	*Tegula*	2	LXXI		-
VINDONISSA	FG57	*Tegula*	10	CIII HI		37.272
VINDONISSA	FG58	*Tegula*	15	LEGXICPF		40.51
VINDONISSA	FG59	*Tegula*	10	CIII HI		1077
VINDONISSA	FG60	*Tegula*	12	LXXIL		-
VINDONISSA	FG61	*Tegula*	10	CIII HI		236
VINDONISSA	FG62	*Tegula*	2	LXXI		23.6378

Annexe C: List of the samples ordered in function of their archaeological site of provenance.

Archeological site of provenance	Analysis n°	Type of object	Stamp-type (Jahn, 1909)	Type of inscription (*Tegulae*) or decoration (*Antefixa*)	Notes	Inventory n°
VINDONISSA	FG63	*Tegula*	2	LXXI		30:2650
VINDONISSA	FG64	*Tegula*	3	LXXISCVI		38:207
VINDONISSA	FG65	*Tegula*	3	LXXISCVI		37:310
VINDONISSA	FG66	*Tegula*	1	LXXI		37:377
VINDONISSA	FG67	*Tegula*	15	LEGXICPF		-
VINDONISSA	FG68	*Tegula*	16	LEGXICPF		33:5650
VINDONISSA	FG69	*Tegula*	15	LEGXICPF		-
VINDONISSA	FG70	*Tegula*	2	LXXI		-
VINDONISSA	FG71	*Tegula*	13	LXXI		turnhalle 911
VINDONISSA	FG72	*Tegula*	5	CVI RAETO		59:1297
VINDONISSA	FG73	*Tegula*	1	LXXI		-
VINDONISSA	FG74	*Tegula*	12	LXXIL		32:7937
VINDONISSA	FG75	*Tegula*	13	LXXI		-
VINDONISSA	FG76	*Tegula*	9	LEGXXI		-
VINDONISSA	FG77	*Tegula*	8	CXXVI		-
VINDONISSA	FG78	*Tegula*	14	LEGXICPF		...75
VINDONISSA	FG79	*Tegula*	14	LEGXICPF		38:77
VINDONISSA	FG80	*Tegula*	14	LEGXICPF		38:97
VINDONISSA	FG81	*Tegula*	14	LEGXICPF		26:973
VINDONISSA	FG83	*Tegula*	4	LXXIC		4:3297
VINDONISSA	FG84	*Tegula*	3	LXXISCVI		38:249
VINDONISSA	FG85	*Tegula*	4	LXXIC		36:97
VINDONISSA	FG86	*Tegula*	4	LXXIC		26:115
VINDONISSA	FG87	*Tegula*	1	LXXI		59:1775
VINDONISSA	FG88	*Tegula*	14	LEGXICPF		2639
VINDONISSA	FG89	*Tegula*	3	LXXISCVI		38:242
VINDONISSA	FG90	*Tegula*	13	LXXI		19.457
VINDONISSA	FG91	*Tegula*	13	LXXI		37:462
VINDONISSA	FG92	*Tegula*	16	LEGXICPF		40:57
VINDONISSA	FG93	*Tegula*	15	LEGXICPF		28:84
VINDONISSA	FG94	*Tegula*	14	LEGXICPF		(293):2821
VINDONISSA	FG95	*Tegula*	13	LXXI		29:471
VINDONISSA	FG96	*Tegula*	12	LXXIL		36:75

Annexe C: List of the samples ordered in function of their archaeological site of provenance.

Archeological site of provenance	Analysis n°	Type of object	Stamp-type (Jahn, 1909)	Type of inscription (*Tegulae*) or decoration (*Antefixa*)	Notes	Inventory n°
VINDONISSA	FG98	*Tegula*	7	CVIIR		59:852
VINDONISSA	FG99	*Tegula*	1	LXXI		23:3803
VINDONISSA	FG100	*Tegula*	9	LEGXXI		37?:...Z/3
VINDONISSA	FG102	*Tegula*	14	LEGXICPF		24:924
VINDONISSA	FG103	*Tegula*	3	LXXISCVI		33:756
VINDONISSA	FG104	*Tegula*	14	LEGXICPF		8806
VINDONISSA	FG105	*Tegula*	4	LXXIC		-
VINDONISSA	FG106	*Tegula*	4	LXXIC		-
VINDONISSA	FG107	*Tegula*	9	LEGXXI		-
VINDONISSA	FG108	*Tegula*	2	LXXI		-
VINDONISSA	FG109	*Tegula*	1	LXXI		-
VINDONISSA	FG110	*Tegula*	6	CVIIR		-
VINDONISSA	FG111	*Tegula*	15	LEGXICPF		15A?
VINDONISSA	FG112	*Tegula*	15	LEGXICPF		-
VINDONISSA	FG113	*Tegula*	15	LEGXICPF		-
VINDONISSA	FG114	*Tegula*	15	LEGXICPF		-
VINDONISSA	FG115	*Tegula*	12? 13?	LXXIL? LXXI?		...:/55
VINDONISSA	FG116	*Tegula*	2	LXXI		59:2008
VINDONISSA	FG117	*Tegula*	2	LXXI		7475
VINDONISSA	FG124	*Antefixum*	NO STAMP	MEDUSA	not analysed	34:5937
VINDONISSA	FG125	*Antefixum*	NO STAMP	MAN	not analysed	-
VINDONISSA	FG126	*Antefixum*	NO STAMP	IUPITER		18:193
VINDONISSA	FG127	*Antefixum*	NO STAMP	WOMAN	not analysed	3857
VINDONISSA	FG128	*Antefixum*	NO STAMP	WOMAN	not analysed	-
VINDONISSA	FG129	*Antefixum*	NO STAMP	EAGLE	not analysed	38:333
VINDONISSA	FG130	*Antefixum*	NO STAMP	PALM		1941:321
VINDONISSA	FG131	*Antefixum*	NO STAMP	PALM		13:968
VINDONISSA	FG132	*Antefixum*	NO STAMP	PALM		-
VINDONISSA	FG133	*Antefixum*	NO STAMP	IUPITER		38:332
VINDONISSA	FG134	*Antefixum*	NO STAMP	PALM		32:1131
VINDONISSA	FG135	*Antefixum*	NO STAMP	MAN		52:730
VINDONISSA	FG136	*Antefixum*	NO STAMP	FLOWER	not analysed	35:3698
VINDONISSA	FG137	*Antefixum*	NO STAMP	FLOWER	not analysed	

Annexe C: List of the samples ordered in function of their archaeological site of provenance.

Archeological site of provenance	Analysis n°	Type of object	Stamp-type (Jahn, 1909)	Type of inscription (*Tegulae*) or decoration (*Antefixa*)	Notes	Inventory n°
VINDONISSA	FG138	*Antefixum*	NO STAMP	EAGLE	not analysed	52:729
VINDONISSA	FG139	*Antefixum*	NO STAMP	WOMAN	not analysed	51:301
VINDONISSA	FG141	*Tegula*	NO STAMP	-	unstamped tile	V97.1/88 17 15
VINDONISSA	FG142	*Tegula*	NO STAMP	-	unstamped tile	V97.1/981.713
VINDONISSA	FG143	*Antefixum*	NO STAMP	EAGLE		32:1174
VINDONISSA	FG160	*Tegula*	4	LXXIC		AG1
VINDONISSA	FG208	Pot	NO STAMP	-		V76/172 11
VINDONISSA	FG209	Pot	NO STAMP	-		V76/171 38
VINDONISSA	FG210	Pot	NO STAMP	-		V76/171 37
VINDONISSA	FG211	Pot	NO STAMP	-		V76/171 36
VINDONISSA	FG212	Pot	NO STAMP	-		V76/171 35
VINDONISSA	FG213	Pot	NO STAMP	-		V76/171 34
VINDONISSA	FG214	Pot	NO STAMP	-		V76/502 7
VINDONISSA	FG215	Pot	NO STAMP	-		V76/227 6
VINDONISSA	FG216	Pot	NO STAMP	-		V76/191 8
VINDONISSA	FG217	Pot	NO STAMP	-		V76/211 2
VINDONISSA	FG218	Pot	NO STAMP	-		V76/211 3
VINDONISSA	FG219	Pot	NO STAMP	-		V76/204 20
VINDONISSA	FG220	Pot	NO STAMP	-	not analysed	V76/170 5

Annexe D: Results of the modal petrographic analyses on a selected group of samples.

Stamp type	Sample	Counts n°	Clay matrix	Quartz	Feldspar	Biotite	Calcite / limestone fragments	Secondary calcite	Epidote	Muscovite	Silt fragm.	Clay pellets	Greywacke fragments	Pores	tot ARFs	TOT
1	FG51	1869	73.2	4.9	2.8	X	1.2	-	tr.	tr.	-	8.9	4.5	4.2	13.4	99.7
1	FG41	1293	70.9	9.7	1.4	X	4.2	-	tr.	tr.	-	7.6	X	4.4	7.6	98.2
2	FG66	1851	77.8	10.7	2.3	X	1.5	-	X	tr.	X	1.8	X	4.1	1.8	98.1
2	FG187	1632	79.4	12.7	1.8	X	-	-	-	tr.	X	1.5	X	3.9	1.5	99.3
2	FG166	1479	79.5	5.5	3.5	-	X	-	-	tr.	5.5	1.0	2.0	3.0	8.5	100.0
2	FG117	1629	82.3	3.4	2.1	X	X	-	X	tr.	-	5.1	2.3	4.1	7.4	99.3
2	FG73	2079	84.3	3.5	1.3	X	X	-	-	tr.	-	4.5	1.4	3.8	5.9	98.8
3	FG184	1620	79.9	8.4	2.2	X	1.7	-	X	X	X	2.6	X	3.4	2.6	98.1
3	FG172	1728	83.3	5.0	X	-	-	-	-	tr.	-	4.7	1.6	4.9	6.2	99.5
3	FG198	1128	89.4	4.5	1.1	X	X	-	X	tr.	-	X	X	2.9	-	97.9
3	FG15	1854	69.9	9.1	3.1	X	2.4	tr.	X	tr.	2.1	4.7	X	7.4	6.8	98.7
4	FG18	1653	87.1	4.5	X	-	-	-	X	tr.	X	1.5	1.6	4.0	3.1	98.7
4	FG106	1824	78.0	13.4	1.5	X	-	-	-	X	X	1.4	1.4	4.0	2.7	99.6
4	FG48	1701	83.6	6.7	X	-	-	-	-	X	1.9	1.2	2.3	2.8	5.5	98.6
4	FG153	1773	81.2	4.2	X	-	3.1	-	-	tr.	2.0	3.4	X	4.7	5.4	98.6
9	FG100	1854	81.4	8.1	1.9	X	X	-	X	X	X	2.3	1.6	3.7	3.9	99.0
9	FG52	2208	79.4	5.6	X	X	2.5	-	X	X	X	8.3	X	2.6	8.3	98.2
9	FG168	1740	81.2	9.5	1.9	-	-	-	-	tr.	X	X	3.3	3.5	3.3	99.3
10	FG57	1566	72.9	9.1	1.6	-	-	-	-	tr.	-	-	13.2	3.1	13.2	99.8
12	FG202	1926	79.0	14.5	1.6	X	X	-	-	X	X	1.3	X	3.0	1.3	99.2
12	FG178	2016	78.6	13.5	1.8	X	X	tr.	X	X	-	X	X	3.0	-	96.9
12	FG60	2109	78.5	16.5	1.1	X	X	-	X	X	-	X	X	1.4	-	97.6
12	FG23	1875	76.8	14.9	1.1	X	X	-	X	1.6	-	X	X	2.9	-	97.3
13	FG91	1836	90.8	4.1	X	X	1.5	tr.	-	X	-	-	-	2.4	-	98.8
13	FG175	1767	90.5	3.6	X	X	2.4	-	X	tr.	-	X	-	2.0	-	98.5
13	FG75	1857	85.8	5.7	X	X	2.1	-	-	X	-	-	-	3.2	-	96.8
14	FG94	1956	82.4	6.9	X	-	-	-	-	tr.	1.4	3.1	2.1	3.7	6.6	99.6
14	FG80	1941	81.6	7.1	X	X	-	-	-	tr.	4.2	1.0	4.2	-	9.4	98.1
14	FG27	1848	76.3	8.1	1.3	-	-	-	X	tr.	1.0	5.8	3.6	3.6	10.4	99.7
15	FG113	1746	83.8	4.6	2.8	X	X	-	X	X	X	X	3.8	2.8	3.8	97.8
15	FG93	2064	79.5	8.1	1.9	X	-	-	X	tr.	2.8	1.5	3.1	3.2	7.3	100.0
15	FG58	1836	70.6	5.9	X	X	-	-	X	tr.	9.2	2.0	10.0	1.8	21.1	99.4
16	FG54	1821	77.9	6.9	X	X	-	-	-	X	1.8	X	6.8	4.3	8.6	97.7
16	FG31	1893	84.6	4.8	1.1	X	-	-	X	X	3.4	2.0	-	4.4	5.4	100.3
16	FG196	1914	82.4	5.0	X	X	-	-	X	tr.	X	5.2	X	5.2	5.2	97.8

X, accessory amount (0.1<X<1 vol%); tr., trace amount (<0.1 vol%); -, absent

Annexe E: Chemical compositions of the analysed clay and ceramic samples.

Clay sample	SiO_2	TiO_2	Al_2O_3	Fe_2O_{3T}	MnO	MgO	CaO	Na_2O	K_2O	P_2O_5	L.O.I.	SUM	Ba	Cr	Cu	Nb	Ni	Pb	Rb	Sr	V	Y	Zn
FG1	78.48	0.64	9.74	3.47	0.04	0.81	0.85	1.47	1.86	0.15	2.29	99.78	304	96	-	22	47	35	73	73	64	42	36
FG2	77.47	0.73	10.03	3.71	0.05	0.75	0.75	1.40	1.57	0.09	3.16	99.69	304	91	-	22	39	33	63	68	68	36	33
FG3	80.26	0.53	9.03	2.79	0.10	0.84	0.66	1.53	1.84	0.13	2.66	100.36	266	79	-	12	28	13	86	70	44	26	55
FG4	69.25	0.56	11.87	3.95	0.10	1.44	3.57	1.55	2.38	0.09	5.53	100.30	330	84	-	10	38	19	120	135	72	29	67
FG5	40.07	0.50	9.71	2.19	0.03	1.22	23.09	0.34	1.82	0.09	21.02	100.08	149	62	-	10	36	24	84	320	88	30	43
FG6	66.05	0.83	14.70	6.70	0.15	1.48	1.02	0.54	2.64	0.16	5.31	99.59	286	119	-	17	90	38	130	64	134	66	98
FG7	74.17	0.70	11.25	3.85	0.15	1.37	0.67	1.24	2.56	0.10	3.84	99.90	321	84	-	25	50	39	96	71	69	38	46
FG8	69.12	0.73	11.72	4.95	0.13	2.28	2.02	1.10	2.05	0.16	5.74	99.99	305	86	-	18	55	38	81	163	82	36	32
FG9	63.85	0.63	9.24	4.60	0.13	2.90	3.97	0.91	1.62	0.27	12.15	100.27	257	83	-	18	45	34	62	79	80	33	45
FG42	73.92	0.69	11.86	4.30	0.11	1.33	0.75	1.37	1.96	0.15	3.42	99.86	349	89	-	17	59	36	92	74	71	37	49
FG43	73.65	0.68	11.97	4.41	0.10	1.31	0.75	1.54	2.17	0.12	3.17	99.85	313	96	-	23	54	31	94	69	76	36	43
FG44	70.65	0.45	7.50	2.72	0.09	1.82	6.16	0.99	1.54	0.12	7.97	100.02	209	75	-	10	28	14	74	107	46	22	44
FG45	73.56	0.71	11.75	4.70	0.12	1.07	0.72	1.12	1.90	0.12	3.83	99.60	313	94	-	24	53	34	91	71	80	36	47
FG46	68.64	0.61	12.64	4.52	0.12	1.44	1.01	1.43	2.30	0.20	7.07	99.99	338	99	-	18	59	15	113	66	76	30	59
FG231	67.36	0.52	8.81	3.26	0.10	2.17	6.45	1.06	1.69	0.14	8.86	100.40	229	73	-	9	36	15	84	115	62	27	57

Ceramic sample	SiO_2	TiO_2	Al_2O_3	Fe_2O_{3T}	MnO	MgO	CaO	Na_2O	K_2O	P_2O_5	L.O.I.	SUM	Ba	Cr	Cu	Nb	Ni	Pb	Rb	Sr	V	Y	Zn
FG10	61.81	0.96	17.63	7.23	0.18	2.87	1.01	1.44	3.85	0.22	2.69	99.91	447	166	27	14	115	44	167	50	110	39	110
FG11	70.44	0.76	14.41	5.32	0.10	1.75	1.07	1.73	2.76	0.30	1.41	100.06	428	108	13	17	74	36	133	85	72	48	87
FG12	65.26	0.71	16.03	6.25	0.13	2.52	1.70	1.55	3.71	0.26	1.64	99.76	371	145	22	15	95	41	152	65	92	31	82
FG13	68.70	0.65	14.69	5.17	0.12	2.05	1.71	2.07	3.37	0.18	1.22	99.93	363	102	16	15	74	41	141	85	81	38	67
FG14	66.97	0.71	15.78	5.91	0.14	2.35	1.39	1.90	3.51	0.31	1.00	99.97	390	106	20	15	79	42	151	82	83	40	82
FG15	63.99	0.74	16.62	6.57	0.16	2.93	1.88	1.47	3.99	0.20	1.46	100.01	405	136	27	15	100	43	176	76	97	37	95
FG16	62.00	0.79	17.24	7.41	0.18	3.04	2.54	1.11	3.19	0.14	2.35	99.99	421	252	48	14	205	34	147	82	127	39	97
FG17	61.03	0.84	18.23	7.73	0.19	3.30	2.10	1.02	3.38	0.13	1.70	99.66	423	269	46	16	218	36	158	67	141	37	94
FG18	61.17	0.83	17.92	7.79	0.19	3.29	2.91	1.05	3.26	0.13	1.56	100.00	381	268	43	14	217	29	155	78	133	39	94
FG19	59.41	0.81	18.41	7.40	0.15	3.58	4.03	1.11	3.49	0.14	1.54	100.07	423	260	44	16	202	34	165	92	142	32	96
FG20	64.29	0.73	16.90	6.69	0.15	2.85	1.19	1.52	4.01	0.12	1.67	100.12	431	150	24	13	103	48	184	56	108	34	91
FG21	66.74	0.70	15.55	5.98	0.13	2.51	1.51	1.71	3.71	0.15	1.34	100.02	376	135	29	15	94	37	157	64	94	36	81
FG22	72.37	0.63	13.20	4.18	0.06	1.59	1.92	1.82	2.82	0.19	1.50	100.27	427	103	10	15	55	33	127	94	62	35	64
FG23	69.87	0.72	14.92	5.82	0.11	1.94	1.19	0.96	2.82	0.39	1.56	100.30	337	119	13	14	80	34	132	69	94	33	69
FG24	70.88	0.73	14.85	5.77	0.11	1.92	0.84	0.93	2.96	0.11	1.09	100.18	342	126	18	19	79	33	143	56	92	30	72
FG25	72.68	0.67	13.67	5.25	0.10	1.70	1.11	1.14	2.75	0.13	1.04	100.24	334	109	18	14	68	33	130	63	84	29	71
FG26	63.08	0.77	16.32	6.66	0.15	3.16	2.76	1.73	3.73	0.26	1.26	99.89	372	142	14	15	106	37	154	83	94	39	86
FG27	67.70	0.75	15.53	6.02	0.14	2.32	1.16	1.54	3.84	0.17	0.92	100.09	430	133	7	16	89	36	147	70	88	40	80
FG28	69.53	0.75	15.11	5.56	0.12	2.21	0.79	1.79	3.22	0.18	0.66	99.91	370	126	7	14	81	36	137	67	75	35	74
FG29	65.54	0.74	16.23	6.73	0.16	2.90	1.18	1.61	3.88	0.32	0.67	99.96	395	140	12	14	99	49	166	63	99	39	95
FG30	63.98	0.75	17.10	6.74	0.16	3.04	1.73	1.44	3.98	0.13	1.32	100.36	411	147	26	17	101	42	182	69	102	35	95
FG31	64.29	0.79	16.25	6.65	0.15	2.94	1.27	1.62	3.42	0.20	1.98	99.56	379	153	5	17	107	37	141	60	92	43	80
FG32	64.12	0.83	17.55	7.21	0.15	3.17	1.07	1.67	3.83	0.23	0.65	100.49	405	159	23	14	112	39	160	62	95	45	93
FG33	72.95	0.68	13.52	5.24	0.11	1.53	0.93	1.17	2.70	0.30	1.32	100.45	352	104	11	17	68	26	119	62	82	27	60
FG34	65.71	0.74	17.07	6.18	0.13	2.51	1.65	1.54	3.74	0.18	0.70	100.15	420	113	25	16	85	41	175	71	107	39	94
FG35	71.40	0.67	13.97	5.08	0.07	1.46	0.97	1.99	2.82	0.25	1.49	100.16	435	94	15	19	60	34	125	72	65	41	69
FG36	71.37	0.66	13.58	5.25	0.11	1.58	1.33	1.09	2.63	0.25	2.34	100.19	332	117	15	16	68	30	118	67	82	32	63
FG37	72.92	0.67	14.99	4.32	0.04	1.46	0.56	1.52	2.77	0.21	0.88	100.33	410	105	4	24	56	36	139	64	79	41	71
FG38	65.48	0.73	17.09	6.20	0.12	2.44	1.43	1.57	3.69	0.21	1.17	100.12	441	117	28	14	81	35	171	73	100	41	93

*, recalculated ($P_2O_5 > 0.5$ wt%); -, below detection limits/not measured

Annexe E: Chemical compositions of the analysed clay and ceramic samples.

Ceramic sample	SiO_2	TiO_2	Al_2O_3	Fe_2O_{3T}	MnO	MgO	CaO	Na_2O	K_2O	P_2O_5	$L.O.I.$	SUM	Ba	Cr	Cu	Nb	Ni	Pb	Rb	Sr	V	Y	Zn
FG39	71.59	0.71	14.87	4.88	0.07	1.67	0.76	1.72	2.95	0.15	0.85	100.22	411	100	3	20	68	39	144	70	72	45	78
FG40	71.90	0.66	14.12	5.06	0.09	1.51	1.08	1.85	2.85	0.32	1.04	100.48	489	96	14	18	62	38	131	79	71	41	72
FG41	62.18	0.71	17.22	6.78	0.12	3.02	2.27	1.31	4.22	0.25	1.95	100.02	416	154	21	14	105	45	179	69	96	38	93
FG47	69.68	0.65	15.18	5.02	0.10	1.86	1.11	1.64	3.31	0.17	1.02	99.74	479	93	6	16	67	32	144	84	79	32	74
FG48	57.81	0.79	17.19	7.28	0.17	3.51	5.72	0.75	3.05	0.28	3.03	99.58	388	260	28	13	201	39	139	112	118	34	78
FG49	69.99	0.65	15.04	5.15	0.13	2.04	1.16	1.37	3.45	0.09	0.72	99.78	456	96	79	15	70	35	137	77	95	34	65
FG50	68.31	0.68	15.26	5.40	0.14	2.15	1.92	1.39	3.20	0.13	1.24	99.82	388	88	21	15	68	40	145	70	86	37	84
FG51	63.75	0.77	17.00	6.50	0.13	2.82	1.78	1.41	3.78	0.22	1.43	99.60	419	140	15	11	97	43	165	74	90	39	81
FG52	62.94	0.75	17.50	6.81	0.13	2.74	1.47	1.27	3.92	0.20	1.92	99.64	438	150	11	15	102	42	172	58	103	36	80
FG53	67.75	0.75	15.58	5.81	0.14	2.42	0.94	1.83	3.47	0.13	0.81	99.65	363	126	10	13	86	37	142	67	85	40	64
FG54	68.57	0.76	15.15	6.21	0.13	2.43	0.79	1.71	3.17	0.14	0.65	99.71	369	135	4	15	83	36	130	59	75	37	65
FG55	64.34	0.74	16.84	6.30	0.13	2.71	1.62	1.62	3.62	0.20	1.59	99.70	398	119	12	18	93	40	164	72	96	41	80
FG56	69.21	0.63	13.72	4.82	0.13	1.97	2.78	1.37	2.84	0.22	2.20	99.88	365	84	5	15	57	32	113	79	71	30	56
FG57	71.18	0.76	14.73	5.40	0.08	1.54	1.05	1.50	2.63	0.48	0.41	99.75	434	104	4	19	66	38	120	80	68	38	169
FG58	58.77	0.74	16.46	6.43	0.15	4.14	5.59	1.24	3.56	0.38	2.24	99.69	403	149	18	13	101	44	138	100	70	38	81
FG59	71.11	0.70	16.23	4.57	0.04	1.66	0.56	1.28	2.65	0.16	0.84	99.79	443	116	4	21	73	44	142	62	80	56	75
FG60	69.93	0.73	14.82	5.89	0.12	1.70	0.89	0.80	2.64	0.40	1.99	99.90	353	127	10	17	87	36	115	63	84	37	59
FG61	70.04	0.70	16.13	4.62	0.04	1.63	0.83	1.35	2.64	0.36	1.25	99.58	451	113	5	21	71	42	143	80	76	50	77
FG62	66.99	0.65	14.65	5.42	0.12	2.30	2.14	1.52	3.37	0.15	2.23	99.55	372	124	5	12	86	38	140	77	88	35	82
FG63	66.99	0.68	15.08	5.73	0.13	2.37	2.34	1.46	3.43	0.15	2.08	100.43	357	130	7	13	88	34	147	87	83	34	65
FG64	63.16	0.79	17.31	7.02	0.14	3.18	1.40	1.24	3.88	0.21	1.34	99.67	385	160	12	17	118	43	158	57	96	41	176
FG65	64.62	0.75	16.50	6.37	0.15	2.72	1.74	1.45	3.58	0.24	1.45	99.56	403	123	15	14	89	43	148	71	83	36	76
FG66	65.67	0.72	16.07	5.98	0.13	2.44	1.99	1.65	3.42	0.36	1.35	99.78	398	103	13	13	81	40	151	91	83	37	76
FG67	66.33	0.77	15.49	6.01	0.15	2.86	1.86	1.71	3.40	0.20	0.88	99.67	365	144	9	21	99	31	134	67	92	39	70
FG68	64.00	0.84	17.31	6.96	0.14	3.14	1.03	1.69	3.67	0.20	0.77	99.75	394	144	13	14	109	48	155	56	103	42	136
FG69	66.89	0.73	15.68	6.39	0.16	2.74	1.02	1.44	3.60	0.17	0.69	99.53	366	137	8	11	93	41	147	52	92	35	73
FG70	68.03	0.72	15.66	5.93	0.14	2.42	0.74	1.62	3.51	0.16	0.76	99.70	352	132	7	11	90	41	144	50	80	38	65
FG71	62.23	0.63	11.59	3.94	0.06	2.91	7.52	0.84	1.95	0.44	7.74	99.84	308	89	4	14	61	30	72	111	58	34	48
FG72	66.31	0.76	16.34	6.01	0.14	2.44	1.38	1.37	3.30	0.31	1.25	99.61	413	100	9	15	72	41	140	73	88	36	75
FG73	64.06	0.78	17.20	6.57	0.14	2.78	1.35	1.55	3.81	0.31	0.96	99.52	412	118	18	14	93	41	166	71	93	47	85
FG74	71.13	0.69	14.04	5.47	0.11	1.84	0.98	0.86	2.79	0.14	0.81	98.88	311	121	3	12	71	35	121	56	92	34	57
FG75	58.51	0.58	10.55	3.73	0.07	3.18	10.04	0.85	1.86	0.30	9.95	99.60	305	92	3	10	51	29	69	154	74	32	40
FG76	68.14	0.70	15.41	5.83	0.13	2.36	1.04	1.58	3.54	0.11	0.88	99.73	351	131	-	10	86	38	145	56	82	33	119
FG77	72.26	0.79	14.33	4.66	0.08	1.58	0.77	1.59	2.89	0.20	0.53	99.60	414	96	4	21	64	36	130	68	72	44	63
FG78	67.76	0.70	15.75	6.08	0.16	2.52	0.81	1.71	3.11	0.18	0.72	99.59	343	144	7	11	97	37	124	63	92	35	164
FG79	69.06	0.74	15.09	5.82	0.13	2.35	0.75	1.60	3.23	0.17	0.68	99.62	358	131	4	11	82	37	127	56	81	31	92
FG80	63.45	0.85	17.95	7.16	0.16	3.21	1.11	1.46	3.51	0.23	1.05	100.14	387	155	8	19	111	39	143	57	93	42	85
FG81	65.82	0.80	16.84	6.63	0.13	2.83	1.07	1.43	3.36	0.18	0.94	100.03	399	154	4	11	91	47	136	54	91	37	58
FG82	69.79	0.65	15.57	5.24	0.12	2.05	1.22	1.48	3.17	0.09	0.24	99.61	459	96	6	13	66	40	134	71	88	34	42
FG83	66.79	0.70	16.84	5.89	0.11	2.23	1.41	1.11	3.33	0.17	0.90	99.47	466	108	6	11	76	43	142	66	102	33	48
FG84	60.88	0.77	18.11	7.08	0.14	3.41	1.96	1.14	4.09	0.24	1.69	99.49	417	166	8	13	114	46	166	54	105	40	67
FG85	68.74	0.67	15.97	5.45	0.11	2.08	1.09	1.33	3.23	0.14	0.79	99.61	465	105	4	17	69	36	135	69	85	34	46
FG86	61.70	0.86	18.70	7.76	0.16	3.36	1.44	1.03	3.47	0.22	1.02	99.71	449	135	4	13	88	46	143	70	122	39	70
FG87	67.18	0.69	15.51	5.76	0.12	2.19	1.79	1.68	3.13	0.23	1.47	99.75	377	105	9	16	79	40	132	88	85	38	52

*, recalculated ($P_2O_5 > 0.5$ wt%); -, below detection limits/not measured

78

Annexe E: Chemical compositions of the analysed clay and ceramic samples.

Ceramic sample	SiO$_2$	TiO$_2$	Al$_2$O$_3$	Fe$_2$O$_{3T}$	MnO	MgO	CaO	Na$_2$O	K$_2$O	P$_2$O$_5$	L.O.I.	SUM	Ba	Cr	Cu	Nb	Ni	Pb	Rb	Sr	V	Y	Zn
FG88	66.46	0.79	16.58	6.53	0.13	2.72	0.71	1.39	3.37	0.12	0.85	99.65	388	142	11	14	88	41	140	51	89	33	53
FG89	61.46	0.81	18.34	7.45	0.15	3.51	1.23	1.17	3.91	0.22	1.29	99.55	407	172	4	13	118	46	155	49	105	41	65
FG90	65.08	0.71	13.37	4.74	0.06	2.62	4.49	0.75	2.15	0.34	5.31	99.61	387	100	4	16	69	40	90	100	84	33	43
FG91	60.37	0.64	12.13	4.05	0.06	3.36	8.71	0.70	1.93	0.24	7.63	99.82	318	85	6	11	58	39	75	122	71	35	41
FG92	66.06	0.72	15.71	5.99	0.13	2.53	2.02	1.39	3.22	0.37	1.48	99.63	387	148	4	13	84	40	131	85	86	34	49
FG93	63.87	0.83	17.67	7.25	0.16	3.08	0.95	1.33	3.62	0.14	0.93	99.83	406	150	4	12	98	48	145	53	108	35	79
FG94	64.63	0.80	17.15	7.21	0.17	3.17	0.87	1.21	3.66	0.19	0.71	99.77	387	156	8	14	107	48	149	36	108	38	63
FG95	65.42	0.64	13.01	4.91	0.09	2.37	4.90	0.64	2.20	0.29	5.33	99.80	342	118	9	9	70	30	90	95	84	34	44
FG96	71.84	0.69	14.09	5.42	0.10	1.57	0.82	0.76	2.44	0.43	1.54	99.70	351	114	8	14	65	38	102	51	70	27	38
FG97	62.75	0.71	17.42	6.78	0.13	2.94	1.91	0.93	4.20	0.17	1.63	99.56	390	150	4	12	99	46	165	49	99	34	59
FG98	70.09	0.67	14.62	5.62	0.10	1.43	1.02	1.52	2.64	0.22	1.63	99.55	471	95	7	16	66	41	112	74	69	41	47
FG99	69.85	0.74	14.91	5.87	0.15	1.80	0.98	1.23	2.96	0.22	0.89	99.61	435	120	4	14	68	42	125	67	69	37	55
FG100	65.46	0.78	16.57	6.52	0.13	2.75	1.27	1.39	3.34	0.19	1.27	99.68	379	129	11	11	88	40	136	64	86	34	56
FG101	63.85	0.78	17.49	7.10	0.15	3.09	1.56	1.21	3.78	0.14	0.46	99.61	390	155	4	12	104	46	161	49	96	38	61
FG102	69.80	0.72	14.73	5.78	0.13	2.26	0.78	1.71	2.98	0.14	0.54	99.56	352	129	12	11	77	35	138	54	78	36	42
FG103	66.72	0.72	15.98	5.88	0.13	2.42	1.46	1.71	3.37	0.23	1.06	99.69	384	114	10	11	74	43	138	65	82	35	49
FG104	64.19	0.80	16.74	6.88	0.16	3.15	1.66	1.50	3.42	0.16	0.85	99.50	373	158	4	12	104	46	142	58	96	43	57
FG105	60.75	0.86	18.77	7.81	0.16	3.41	1.98	0.98	3.45	0.20	1.18	99.54	422	131	8	13	91	48	140	73	122	39	71
FG106	68.14	0.67	16.15	5.49	0.10	2.12	1.47	1.32	3.26	0.17	0.79	99.68	479	100	9	13	71	43	140	73	89	34	53
FG107	66.42	0.74	16.32	6.36	0.13	2.62	1.04	1.49	3.42	0.24	1.03	99.82	369	144	4	15	90	38	141	48	90	34	52
FG108	68.96	0.69	15.12	5.34	0.12	2.19	1.39	1.80	3.12	0.12	0.89	99.75	350	109	12	12	70	39	127	70	71	34	41
FG109	62.29	0.81	18.32	7.16	0.14	2.93	1.28	1.44	3.65	0.28	1.25	99.55	450	130	10	16	97	51	162	61	102	43	68
FG110	73.04	0.66	13.61	4.40	0.07	1.33	0.85	1.65	2.50	0.44	1.10	99.64	453	87	8	12	57	38	108	67	61	35	41
FG111	64.92	0.74	16.25	6.69	0.16	3.10	1.61	1.34	3.51	0.19	0.97	99.48	389	138	9	14	92	44	148	48	92	39	57
FG112	65.97	0.73	16.48	6.44	0.14	2.91	1.23	1.28	3.58	0.13	0.83	99.73	389	146	4	12	93	45	151	54	100	36	59
FG113	66.65	0.76	15.68	6.23	0.16	2.78	1.23	1.63	3.09	0.20	0.91	99.33	332	150	8	16	92	32	115	53	91	40	50
FG114	65.47	0.74	16.65	6.32	0.14	2.99	1.31	1.34	3.57	0.14	0.86	99.53	392	148	13	13	97	41	153	53	89	35	57
FG115	66.04	0.69	15.18	5.93	0.13	2.31	2.48	0.45	2.40	0.31	3.75	99.67	322	138	12	13	90	35	104	78	89	38	43
FG116	67.15	0.79	16.33	6.65	0.13	2.60	0.95	1.45	3.10	0.21	0.18	99.53	389	142	8	14	90	46	141	51	93	41	60
FG117	61.51	0.76	18.26	7.29	0.14	3.21	1.62	0.98	3.95	0.23	1.69	99.64	410	161	7	11	108	42	166	47	102	36	64
FG118	67.18	0.82	15.97	6.43	0.13	2.69	1.14	1.86	3.00	0.13	0.36	99.70	340	154	4	19	89	38	121	49	94	37	60
FG119	67.90	0.78	15.85	5.98	0.13	2.37	1.21	1.85	3.20	0.15	0.58	100.00	352	134	6	19	77	38	134	61	81	35	48
FG120	67.92	0.79	16.36	6.18	0.14	2.29	0.81	1.45	3.07	0.11	0.68	99.81	391	113	18	15	72	40	131	49	82	30	68
FG121	64.51	0.80	16.69	6.72	0.15	3.45	2.28	1.49	3.53	0.14	0.14	99.88	380	146	11	21	93	47	146	55	89	35	48
FG122	68.23	0.75	15.46	6.36	0.15	2.57	0.79	1.56	3.21	0.16	0.59	99.83	355	129	24	18	83	42	126	39	76	34	63
FG123	65.12	0.84	16.89	7.24	0.18	3.07	0.75	1.39	3.41	0.18	0.65	99.72	352	161	4	17	102	42	136	33	91	39	53
FG126	71.98	0.57	12.37	4.64	0.06	1.40	2.57	1.62	2.31	0.28	1.98	99.78	448	105	789	11	44	18	122	109	61	31	89
FG130	66.10	0.80	16.31	6.56	0.16	2.06	1.67	1.25	2.80	0.27	1.56	99.53	473	127	88	18	67	29	163	94	94	39	125
FG131	67.36	0.76	15.57	6.36	0.19	1.92	1.72	1.27	2.80	0.35	1.56	99.86	481	117	47	16	64	31	164	95	96	38	120
FG132	68.14	0.76	15.42	6.14	0.19	1.89	1.36	1.30	2.78	0.36	1.22	99.55	489	113	37	16	61	29	166	96	88	37	113
FG133*	69.25	0.67	14.14	5.61	0.07	1.50	1.90	1.51	2.26	0.20	2.48	99.59	435	128	37	14	54	21	98	108	56	38	106
FG134	66.28	0.83	16.64	6.66	0.18	2.06	1.02	1.21	2.67	0.45	1.58	99.58	465	131	31	18	68	27	146	93	82	39	122
FG135*	71.58	0.61	13.29	4.96	0.08	1.42	2.09	1.64	2.28	0.20	1.65	99.81	498	115	110	13	50	18	119	108	66	37	92
FG140	67.25	0.80	15.75	6.12	0.14	2.67	1.22	1.87	3.13	0.16	0.68	99.79	350	139	12	18	90	35	118	53	94	35	57
FG141*	70.54	0.79	14.24	5.74	0.06	1.80	2.26	0.84	2.21	0.20	1.31	99.99	422	128	21	15	69	22	129	132	96	36	164
FG142	68.69	0.79	15.03	6.12	0.07	2.39	2.37	0.65	2.27	0.27	1.07	99.72	370	140	25	17	80	25	139	99	100	36	173

*, recalculated (P2O5>0.5wt%); -, below detection limits/not measured

Annexe E: Chemical compositions of the analysed clay and ceramic samples.

Ceramic sample	SiO$_2$	TiO$_2$	Al$_2$O$_3$	Fe$_2$O$_{3T}$	MnO	MgO	CaO	Na$_2$O	K$_2$O	P$_2$O$_5$	L.O.I.	SUM	Ba	Cr	Cu	Nb	Ni	Pb	Rb	Sr	V	Y	Zn
FG143	66.15	0.71	15.97	5.73	0.13	2.52	1.69	1.69	3.57	0.17	1.23	99.55	372	116	41	14	72	30	176	86	100	38	109
FG144	64.15	0.78	17.02	6.43	0.14	3.02	2.13	1.14	3.43	0.15	1.34	99.73	432	122	38	17	70	33	170	98	118	37	115
FG145	69.62	0.64	15.28	5.05	0.10	1.91	1.03	1.59	3.39	0.25	1.04	99.90	517	94	24	13	55	28	161	95	84	35	94
FG146	60.42	0.85	18.61	7.80	0.16	3.89	2.56	0.74	3.30	0.19	1.47	99.99	427	276	54	15	223	30	168	82	141	35	113
FG147	63.30	0.80	17.36	7.17	0.17	3.05	2.01	1.25	3.55	0.14	1.23	100.04	413	120	42	18	73	40	161	94	111	38	111
FG148	64.59	0.79	17.40	7.11	0.15	2.92	1.13	1.17	3.57	0.17	1.07	100.07	447	185	46	17	110	49	163	81	109	36	112
FG149	62.44	0.83	18.20	7.53	0.14	3.35	1.89	0.72	3.30	0.10	1.56	100.05	400	267	46	16	213	50	162	73	134	35	114
FG150*	67.18	0.68	16.22	5.60	0.13	1.92	1.22	1.60	3.34	0.20	1.76	99.84	690	176	29	15	113	31	157	106	83	37	87
FG151	70.44	0.62	15.16	4.85	0.10	1.75	1.12	1.83	3.35	0.11	0.96	100.30	471	83	23	14	50	31	156	101	67	34	73
FG152	61.61	0.79	17.64	7.44	0.20	3.32	3.02	0.79	3.13	0.11	2.20	100.25	406	254	49	15	214	25	156	87	128	36	112
FG153	59.82	0.80	17.71	7.49	0.16	3.55	4.59	0.79	3.09	0.29	1.58	99.85	403	273	54	16	219	29	163	113	141	32	109
FG154	60.00	0.86	18.42	7.86	0.16	3.35	2.67	0.70	3.27	0.09	2.17	99.54	400	254	58	18	206	27	165	88	128	34	113
FG155*	61.18	0.86	18.46	8.02	0.20	3.25	1.51	1.06	3.56	0.20	1.56	99.85	560	127	47	18	84	32	167	107	119	40	131
FG156	58.00	0.83	18.27	7.37	0.16	3.48	5.59	1.01	3.43	0.34	1.32	99.79	450	128	46	16	80	34	166	189	119	42	130
FG157	63.05	0.83	17.95	7.44	0.18	3.13	1.34	1.16	3.52	0.18	1.35	100.12	454	126	44	16	78	34	167	88	111	38	121
FG158	64.28	0.78	17.06	7.55	0.15	3.56	1.59	0.71	3.00	0.09	0.88	99.65	344	319	41	17	280	25	161	66	131	35	103
FG159	59.34	0.79	17.76	7.46	0.16	3.60	4.55	0.80	3.09	0.11	2.25	99.90	428	258	50	15	209	28	160	125	123	30	105
FG160	70.27	0.64	15.24	5.11	0.10	1.97	0.94	1.56	3.31	0.11	0.81	100.06	488	90	24	15	58	28	152	86	77	32	79
FG161	67.10	0.74	16.20	6.05	0.13	2.46	0.91	1.61	3.42	0.20	1.24	100.05	401	117	94	16	78	37	163	73	77	40	116
FG162	64.92	0.76	16.97	6.74	0.14	2.95	0.87	1.40	3.64	0.12	1.44	99.94	376	151	34	16	103	37	161	58	88	37	112
FG163	68.75	0.67	15.36	5.50	0.14	2.40	1.01	1.53	3.37	0.09	1.07	99.90	385	136	20	14	79	28	152	65	70	30	84
FG164	65.22	0.79	16.68	6.58	0.15	2.91	1.19	1.57	3.34	0.16	1.38	99.96	386	159	32	16	104	34	150	80	88	37	101
FG165	64.70	0.78	17.43	6.69	0.15	2.72	0.92	1.41	3.57	0.21	1.38	99.94	432	117	36	16	78	36	170	72	73	38	115
FG166	65.92	0.75	16.90	6.35	0.14	2.60	0.81	1.60	3.41	0.17	1.41	100.05	385	121	31	16	82	40	158	67	74	41	111
FG167	66.56	0.71	16.08	5.97	0.13	2.44	1.60	1.69	3.41	0.15	1.58	100.33	371	112	26	17	75	37	160	81	81	41	100
FG168	67.78	0.70	15.71	6.01	0.15	2.47	1.16	1.57	3.37	0.12	1.20	100.23	370	130	104	14	81	30	157	65	82	32	90
FG169	65.80	0.80	16.69	6.68	0.15	2.96	1.00	1.58	3.46	0.13	1.10	100.34	384	156	226	16	104	31	152	63	86	36	106
FG170	67.04	0.75	15.61	6.04	0.14	2.46	1.69	1.79	3.17	0.17	1.43	100.30	391	141	37	12	92	30	150	92	93	32	92
FG171	62.74	0.86	18.07	7.36	0.13	3.29	0.63	1.26	3.82	0.09	1.26	99.51	399	164	35	15	107	33	180	55	109	31	115
FG172	64.66	0.78	17.41	6.97	0.16	3.06	0.94	1.38	3.86	0.14	0.80	100.16	422	143	39	15	95	48	185	67	90	38	119
FG173	65.92	0.76	16.88	6.64	0.15	2.84	0.70	1.19	3.57	0.10	1.29	100.05	394	145	40	15	93	32	165	53	86	31	103
FG174	70.70	0.68	13.98	5.43	0.10	1.73	1.49	0.74	2.62	0.08	2.30	99.85	324	113	21	14	69	19	136	75	89	27	154
FG175	60.48	0.61	11.23	3.58	0.05	3.28	9.50	0.87	1.82	0.16	8.50	100.08	286	91	21	14	52	16	84	198	78	32	136
FG176	70.52	0.72	14.57	5.69	0.11	1.95	1.24	0.71	2.75	0.08	1.51	99.84	318	122	24	15	70	22	151	77	88	28	151
FG177	70.92	0.71	15.02	5.89	0.11	1.89	1.31	0.72	2.76	0.08	1.97	101.37	331	123	22	15	74	22	144	78	100	28	300
FG178	71.00	0.71	14.57	5.76	0.11	1.98	1.13	0.78	2.78	0.10	1.06	99.98	324	122	40	15	74	22	149	66	101	34	154
FG179	70.56	0.73	14.84	5.74	0.11	1.88	1.18	0.70	2.79	0.08	1.47	100.08	328	118	29	13	73	23	150	75	101	29	161
FG180	71.02	0.71	14.76	5.80	0.11	2.02	1.22	0.76	2.76	0.10	1.12	100.38	322	121	33	13	75	22	150	69	96	31	153
FG181	70.94	0.71	14.81	5.84	0.11	2.00	0.99	0.75	2.82	0.10	0.90	99.97	324	127	29	13	74	20	151	62	100	31	153
FG182	69.97	0.70	14.25	5.65	0.11	1.91	1.94	0.74	2.65	0.14	1.80	99.84	327	121	30	15	75	20	141	107	96	34	156
FG183	66.47	0.76	16.13	6.39	0.14	2.68	0.88	1.52	3.46	0.10	0.94	99.46	378	145	19	16	88	23	162	62	90	32	164
FG184	68.02	0.72	15.95	5.89	0.14	2.39	1.10	1.72	3.52	0.16	0.89	100.50	385	108	28	16	69	30	165	78	77	38	172
FG185	66.53	0.75	16.35	6.19	0.14	2.57	0.98	1.69	3.58	0.17	0.81	99.75	385	118	33	17	74	34	174	70	88	41	176
FG186	64.04	0.78	17.53	7.14	0.16	3.11	0.78	1.15	4.00	0.14	0.93	99.76	394	159	33	12	108	30	186	50	97	42	181
FG187	68.59	0.70	15.68	5.66	0.15	2.29	0.80	1.35	3.21	0.20	1.28	99.90	395	97	30	15	59	27	150	56	88	35	169

*, recalculated (P2O5>0.5wt%); -, below detection limits/not measured

Annexe E: Chemical compositions of the analysed clay and ceramic samples.

Ceramic sample	SiO$_2$	TiO$_2$	Al$_2$O$_3$	Fe$_2$O$_{3T}$	MnO	MgO	CaO	Na$_2$O	K$_2$O	P$_2$O$_5$	L.O.I.	SUM	Ba	Cr	Cu	Nb	Ni	Pb	Rb	Sr	V	Y	Zn
FG188	64.21	0.72	16.26	6.47	0.14	2.82	2.24	1.22	3.81	0.15	1.75	99.78	380	141	29	12	96	24	175	77	101	38	174
FG189	65.87	0.71	15.85	5.89	0.13	2.48	1.90	1.62	3.49	0.16	1.64	99.73	362	109	29	16	74	28	170	82	84	38	176
FG190	60.63	0.78	17.94	7.48	0.15	3.98	2.74	0.69	3.15	0.17	1.95	99.65	383	314	42	15	262	22	163	95	136	35	182
FG191	65.36	0.75	16.42	6.29	0.15	2.67	1.59	1.68	3.49	0.21	1.42	100.02	379	126	32	14	81	30	172	77	85	41	183
FG193	67.66	0.70	15.61	5.81	0.13	2.39	1.12	1.64	3.46	0.17	0.85	99.53	380	103	22	16	71	29	166	75	76	39	173
FG194	64.41	0.75	16.55	6.44	0.15	3.24	1.89	1.44	3.70	0.17	0.87	99.62	397	148	36	15	91	26	169	73	93	36	179
FG195	61.82	0.82	17.64	7.20	0.17	3.52	1.47	1.40	3.77	0.37	1.33	99.52	410	150	39	16	104	34	173	63	106	45	195
FG196	72.64	0.68	13.67	5.32	0.10	1.73	0.85	0.88	2.66	0.10	1.09	99.72	321	114	17	14	66	17	138	60	85	27	146
FG197	63.41	0.74	17.56	6.22	0.11	2.51	2.52	1.02	3.60	0.18	1.67	99.53	450	116	31	14	70	29	179	119	110	32	184
FG198	69.25	0.71	15.11	6.18	0.12	2.24	0.87	1.11	2.83	0.18	0.88	99.50	369	144	13	14	73	21	145	73	102	38	171
FG199	69.06	0.68	15.25	5.78	0.12	2.31	0.78	1.60	3.37	0.16	0.74	99.86	352	125	29	14	78	24	158	63	79	34	158
FG200	66.39	0.65	13.10	4.88	0.10	2.47	4.44	0.74	2.32	0.12	4.84	100.06	292	118	32	12	71	20	119	112	89	34	147
FG201	72.33	0.67	13.75	5.38	0.10	1.82	1.24	0.84	2.66	0.11	1.10	99.99	322	117	23	12	65	17	136	67	93	28	147
FG202	71.60	0.70	14.59	5.80	0.11	1.96	0.86	0.76	2.78	0.11	0.76	100.05	311	131	27	15	73	22	143	63	90	33	153
FG203	66.82	0.70	13.05	4.43	0.06	2.56	4.17	0.84	2.21	0.15	4.64	99.63	313	106	28	15	64	18	109	108	92	34	159
FG204	70.78	0.72	14.92	5.84	0.11	2.01	0.95	0.72	2.85	0.10	0.87	99.88	314	128	25	15	75	21	151	65	103	30	156
FG205	70.31	0.69	14.51	5.67	0.11	1.94	1.56	0.74	2.73	0.09	1.66	100.02	322	126	26	13	72	26	144	79	102	30	154
FG206	70.63	0.71	14.75	5.83	0.11	2.00	1.17	0.74	2.81	0.10	1.04	99.88	325	123	27	15	74	20	147	77	100	31	153
FG207	72.71	0.70	14.05	5.51	0.11	1.84	0.78	0.82	2.75	0.10	0.69	100.06	322	116	24	14	67	22	145	64	96	27	150
FG208	69.22	0.64	14.05	5.25	0.09	1.52	3.59	1.03	2.48	0.45	1.06	99.39	377	108	-	13	53	22	126	144	79	34	174
FG209	66.87	0.71	15.79	5.62	0.11	2.17	2.36	1.27	3.07	0.26	1.18	99.42	443	106	-	17	57	38	161	109	95	35	178
FG210	70.29	0.60	13.91	4.82	0.09	1.66	3.32	1.21	2.68	0.26	0.86	99.69	414	104	-	14	45	22	143	133	76	32	163
FG211	70.96	0.60	13.78	4.63	0.06	1.66	3.38	1.21	2.65	0.17	0.60	99.70	373	99	-	13	48	24	141	125	71	31	145
FG212	69.05	0.62	14.25	5.39	0.09	1.77	3.12	1.12	2.74	0.21	1.21	99.57	403	110	-	12	53	22	145	114	82	32	86
FG213	67.24	0.66	15.64	5.93	0.15	1.94	3.40	0.95	2.90	0.22	0.89	99.92	390	120	-	14	67	31	154	120	99	46	157
FG214	70.07	0.68	14.77	5.03	0.07	2.20	1.13	1.89	3.17	0.17	0.68	99.85	424	132	-	14	72	22	151	91	79	27	103
FG215	69.12	0.93	17.23	6.25	0.04	1.01	0.82	0.35	2.73	0.19	1.07	99.74	519	110	-	26	46	44	199	86	113	46	195
FG216	66.39	0.67	14.92	5.98	0.11	1.56	4.84	0.97	2.50	0.27	1.26	99.46	348	127	-	15	57	23	130	163	100	39	188
FG217*	57.93	1.06	22.55	11.50	0.21	0.71	1.42	0.39	1.20	0.20	2.77	99.94	352	185	-	29	158	25	71	100	107	143	297
FG218	67.08	0.65	14.85	5.82	0.10	1.57	4.62	1.00	2.51	0.22	1.23	99.65	330	122	-	15	59	19	131	151	99	40	105
FG219	67.81	0.70	16.42	5.95	0.08	2.10	0.89	1.33	3.10	0.22	0.83	99.44	457	134	-	15	69	26	172	74	93	43	187
FG221*	43.83	0.76	16.76	5.58	0.10	2.87	12.38	0.30	1.94	0.20	15.22	99.94	598	105	-	16	71	20	99	236	104	33	181
FG222*	57.94	0.92	21.18	4.97	0.03	2.71	1.27	0.16	7.71	0.20	2.86	99.94	704	154	-	14	96	16	252	94	122	44	225
FG223*	59.51	0.91	21.08	4.98	0.03	2.70	0.80	0.24	7.64	0.20	1.85	99.94	670	154	-	14	96	23	250	68	130	34	214
FG224	61.53	0.87	20.67	4.75	0.03	2.51	0.35	0.19	8.33	0.16	0.02	99.40	411	159	-	15	91	20	275	29	149	30	187
FG225	67.90	0.92	17.70	5.80	0.04	1.58	0.72	0.44	2.47	0.48	1.57	99.61	539	122	-	21	54	36	142	80	106	49	176
FG226	72.70	0.75	13.46	5.51	0.10	1.27	1.43	1.02	2.64	0.34	1.07	100.28	469	109	22	15	122	27	121	150	69	37	166
FG227	74.50	0.72	13.28	4.97	0.09	1.21	1.14	1.33	2.25	0.15	0.71	100.36	407	92	37	14	79	28	107	127	77	35	80
FG228	73.10	1.30	13.00	6.22	0.14	0.82	0.77	0.49	2.22	0.21	1.93	100.19	489	151	12	32	97	26	94	109	68	33	163

*, recalculated (P2O5>0.5wt%); -, below detection limits/not measured

Annexe E: Chemical compositions of the analysed clay and ceramic samples.

Contaminated samples, original compositions

Ceramic sample	SiO$_2$	TiO$_2$	Al$_2$O$_3$	Fe$_2$O$_{3T}$	MnO	MgO	CaO	Na$_2$O	K$_2$O	P$_2$O$_5$	L.O.I.	SUM	Ba	Cr	Cu	Nb	Ni	Pb	Rb	Sr	V	Y	Zn
FG133	68.90	0.66	14.07	5.58	0.07	1.49	1.89	1.50	2.25	0.79	2.48	99.69	435	128	37	14	54	21	98	108	56	38	106
FG135	71.08	0.61	13.20	4.93	0.08	1.41	2.08	1.63	2.26	0.58	1.65	99.50	498	115	110	13	50	18	119	108	66	37	92
FG141	69.93	0.78	14.12	5.69	0.06	1.79	2.24	0.83	2.19	1.00	1.31	99.94	422	128	-	15	69	22	129	132	96	36	164
FG150	67.24	0.68	16.23	5.61	0.13	1.93	1.22	1.60	3.34	0.56	1.76	100.29	690	176	29	15	113	31	157	106	83	37	87
FG155	60.98	0.86	18.40	7.99	0.20	3.24	1.51	1.05	3.54	0.54	1.56	99.87	560	127	47	18	84	32	167	107	119	40	131
FG217	57.09	1.04	22.22	11.33	0.20	0.70	1.40	0.39	1.19	1.05	2.73	99.35	352	185	-	29	158	25	71	100	107	143	297
FG221	43.03	0.75	16.46	5.47	0.09	2.81	12.16	0.30	1.90	1.59	14.94	99.51	598	105	-	16	71	20	99	236	104	33	181
FG222	56.89	0.90	20.80	4.88	0.03	2.66	1.24	0.16	7.57	1.55	2.81	99.49	704	154	-	14	96	16	252	94	122	44	225
FG223	58.76	0.90	20.81	4.92	0.03	2.67	0.79	0.24	7.54	0.86	1.83	99.34	670	154	-	14	96	23	250	68	130	34	214

*, recalculated (P2O5>0.5wt%); -, below detection limits/not measured

Annexe F: Results of the porosimetric analyses on selected representative samples

Sample ID	Stamp type	Total intrusion volume (ml/g)	Total pore area (m2/g)	Average pore diameter (mm)	Bulk density (g/ml)	Apparent (skeletal) density (ml/g)	Porosity (vol%)
FG10	1	0.26	9.00	0.11	1.61	2.74	41.40
FG11	1 b	0.18	2.10	0.35	1.84	2.79	33.99
FG12	2 c/d	0.18	5.15	0.14	1.75	2.57	32.10
FG13	2 C	0.12	0.68	0.72	1.47	1.80	18.18
FG14	3	0.19	1.79	0.42	1.81		33.98
FG15	3E	0.17	2.29	0.30	2.18	3.45	36.93
FG16	4	0.18	3.75	0.19	1.84	2.72	32.59
FG17	4	0.11	1.30	0.33	2.77	3.97	30.19
FG18	4	0.13	1.19	0.44	1.89	2.51	24.84
FG19	4	0.15	1.50	0.40	1.59	2.08	23.86
FG20	9	0.20	4.07	0.20	1.85	2.98	37.88
FG21	9	0.20	1.50	0.55	1.75	2.74	35.90
FG22	11	0.18	1.69	0.42	1.72	2.49	30.75
FG23	12	0.16	3.94	0.17	1.80	2.55	29.57
FG24	12	0.15	2.75	0.23	1.90	2.69	29.34
FG25	12? 13?	0.18	3.34	0.21	1.83	2.70	32.26
FG27	14	0.22	2.64	0.33	1.70	2.69	36.66
FG28	15	0.21	2.30	0.35	1.67	2.58	35.15
FG29	15	0.24	8.18	0.12	1.68	2.78	39.62
FG30	16C	0.21	3.09	0.27	1.67	2.57	35.02
FG31	16C	0.23	2.22	0.41	1.65	2.65	37.81
FG32	16	0.20	2.71	0.30	1.74	2.68	35.04
FG33	12? 13?	0.14	8.22	0.07	1.79	2.39	24.76
FG34	5	0.18	1.20	0.59	1.75	2.54	31.00
FG35	6	0.19	13.40	0.06	1.85	2.82	34.34
FG36	12	0.17	19.00	0.04	1.88	2.78	32.19
FG37	10	0.21	3.83	0.21	1.63	2.46	33.64
FG38	5	0.20	3.66	0.22	1.71	2.61	34.49
FG39	8	0.19	4.19	0.18	1.73	2.58	33.16
FG40	7	0.19	5.65	0.13	1.79	2.68	33.41
FG47	4	0.17	4.43	0.15	1.81	2.64	31.04
FG48	4	0.17	5.10	0.14	1.80	2.60	31.10
FG49	4	0.16	0.80	0.81	1.95	2.86	31.83
FG50	5	0.19	2.26	0.33	1.77	2.63	32.68
FG51	1	0.20	2.51	0.32	1.72	2.62	34.60
FG52	9	0.22	6.73	0.13	1.72	2.76	37.74
FG53	16	0.27	1.07	1.01	1.58	2.76	42.83
FG54	16	0.23	2.28	0.40	1.65	2.64	37.78
FG55	9	0.20	6.15	0.13	1.70	2.58	34.38
FG57	10	0.22	6.84	0.13	1.73	2.76	37.22
FG58	15	0.29	5.89	0.20	1.50	2.65	43.32
FG61	10	0.20	7.53	0.11	1.70	2.60	34.40
FG62	2	0.18	4.24	0.16	1.81	2.59	30.25
FG63	2	0.17	3.30	0.21	1.90	2.81	32.52
FG64	3	0.20	5.50	0.15	1.69	2.57	34.10
FG65	3	0.21	3.41	0.24	1.68	2.58	34.84
FG66	1	0.21	1.94	0.43	1.77	2.78	36.49
FG67	15	0.28	1.42	0.80	1.56	2.80	44.18
FG68	16	0.21	2.22	0.38	1.71	2.67	36.05
FG69	15	0.20	0.92	0.86	1.73	2.63	34.24
FG70	2	0.21	1.65	0.50	1.78	2.80	36.49
FG71	13	0.17	10.11	0.07	1.79	2.60	31.06
FG72	5	0.18	5.31	0.13	1.78	2.61	31.86
FG73	1	0.21	2.37	0.36	1.66	2.54	34.88
FG74	12	0.17	1.19	0.56	1.90	2.78	31.58
FG75	13	0.15	7.08	0.08	1.89	2.62	27.83
FG76	9	0.20	1.46	0.54	1.73	2.63	34.04
FG77	8	0.21	0.99	0.84	1.69	2.59	34.85
FG78	14	0.24	2.69	0.35	1.69	2.79	39.66
FG79	14	0.22	2.09	0.42	1.73	2.76	37.49
FG80	14	0.24	6.18	0.15	1.62	2.63	38.28
FG81	14	0.21	2.64	0.32	1.73	2.76	37.21
FG83	4	0.13	0.90	0.58	2.04	2.78	26.71
FG84	3	0.23	3.96	0.23	1.75	2.89	39.52
FG86	4	0.18	2.29	0.31	1.79	2.61	31.63

Sample ID	Stamp type	Total intrusion volume (ml/g)	Total pore area (m2/g)	Average pore diameter (mm)	Bulk density (g/ml)	Apparent (skeletal) density (ml/g)	Porosity (vol%)
FG87	1	0.21	2.98	0.29	1.72	2.73	36.95
FG90	13	0.14	10.40	0.05	1.92	2.64	27.24
FG91	13	0.16	8.60	0.07	1.71	2.35	27.04
FG92	16	0.21	7.95	0.11	1.79	2.87	37.52
FG93	15	0.22	1.37	0.64	1.76	2.86	38.46
FG94	14	0.24	1.48	0.66	1.73	2.98	41.90
FG95	13	0.14	7.20	0.08	1.84	2.46	25.10
FG96	12	0.18	18.02	0.04	1.75	2.58	31.99
FG99	1	0.21	1.88	0.45	1.69	2.61	35.40
FG100	9	0.20	3.62	0.22	1.72	2.64	34.78
FG102	14	0.20	0.89	0.92	1.77	2.77	36.12
FG103	3	0.18	1.26	0.58	1.78	2.62	32.12
FG104	14	0.24	1.44	0.66	1.63	2.67	38.89
FG105	4	0.22	3.36	0.26	1.72	2.75	37.29
FG106	4	0.16	1.12	0.57	1.92	2.77	30.77
FG107	9	0.19	1.55	0.48	1.84	2.80	34.26
FG109	1	0.22	5.02	0.18	1.73	2.78	37.94
FG110	6	0.18	5.02	0.14	1.78	2.63	32.30
FG111	15	0.25	1.94	0.51	1.66	2.80	40.73
FG112	15	0.20	1.15	0.68	1.72	2.60	33.73
FG113	15	0.26	1.08	0.96	1.53	2.51	39.68
FG114	15	0.21	2.04	0.41	1.76	2.79	36.86
FG116	2	0.07	0.42	0.65	2.17	2.55	14.82
FG118	14	0.06	0.22	1.12	2.24	2.59	13.60
FG119	3?	0.10	0.39	0.99	2.00	2.47	19.22
FG120	2	0.21	4.44	0.19	1.76	2.77	36.55
FG122	15	0.16	0.38	1.73	1.84	2.64	30.17
FG123	14	0.23	1.13	0.80	1.61	2.53	36.44
FG158	4	0.16	2.90	0.22	1.95	2.84	31.22
FG159	4	0.16	2.90	0.22	1.95	2.84	31.22
FG160	4	0.17	2.13	0.31	1.88	2.74	31.30
FG161	2	0.24	4.23	0.22	1.59	2.54	37.53
FG164	15A	0.21	1.97	0.43	1.74	2.77	37.01
FG165	1	0.21	4.35	0.20	1.71	2.68	36.26
FG167	2C/D	0.20	1.40	0.58	1.65	2.47	33.38
FG169	16	0.22	1.65	0.53	1.70	2.70	37.13
FG171	14F2	0.20	10.01	0.08	1.84	2.98	38.13
FG172	3	0.25	5.96	0.17	1.58	2.64	40.17
FG173	3	0.20	4.14	0.20	1.67	2.51	33.42

www.ingramcontent.com/pod-product-compliance
Lightning Source LLC
Chambersburg PA
CBHW061302270326
41932CB00029B/3447

* 9 7 8 1 8 4 1 7 1 8 8 5 9 *